Contents

iii

Contents

iv

Seminar Studies in History

Introduction

Seminar Studies in History offer clearly written, authoritative and stimulating introductions to important topics. They cover major themes in British and European history. The authors are acknowledged experts in their field and the books are works of scholarship in their own right as well as providing a survey of current historical interpretations. They are regularly updated to take account of the latest research.

The material is carefully selected to give the reader sufficient confidence to handle different aspects of the theme as well as being enjoyable and interesting to read.

Seminar Studies in History were the creation of Patrick Richardson, a gifted and original teacher who died tragically in an accident in 1979. The continuing vitality of the series is a tribute to his vision.

Structure of the Book

Each title has a brief introduction or background to the subject, a substantial section of analysis, followed by an assessment, a selection of documents which enable the reader to see how historical judgements are reached and to question and challenge them, a glossary which explains key terms, and a bibliography which provides a guide to further reading.

Throughout the book references are made to the Bibliography, to the relevant document within the Documents section (in Part 7), and to definitions in the Glossary. These are indicated as follows:

- **Bibliography** – a bold number in round brackets (**6**) in the text refers to the corresponding entry in the Bibliography
- **Document** – a bold number in square brackets, preceded by 'doc.' [**doc. 4**] refers to the document in

Introduction

• **Glossary**

the Documents section which relates to/illuminates the passage/idea

– an asterisk after a word* indicates an idea or word which is explained in the Glossary.

Acknowledgements

We are grateful to the Controller of Her Majesty's Stationery Office for the permission to reproduce extracts from the English translation of *Documents on German Foreign Policy.* The map on page 68 is adapted from a map entitled 'High Tide of Nazi Power, End of 1942' (p. 109) from *The Ordeal of Total War 1939–1945* by Gordon Wright. Copyright © 1968 by Gordon Wright. Reprinted by permission of Harper & Row, Publishers, Inc.

Part One: The Background

1 The Setting

Innumerable books and monographs have been written on the origins of the Third Reich. Attempts to define the nature of National Socialism began almost as soon as it became a major political force and have continued ever since. Key issues in this complex and continuing debate are whether Nazism was a variant of Fascism or totalitarianism or in fact essentially a movement which developed out of the unique course of German history (**59, 163**).

The orthodox Marxist view, which dominated the thinking of historians in Russia and eastern Europe until the late 1980s, was that Nazism, as a species of Fascism, was indeed a 'terrorist dictatorship of the most reactionary, most Chauvinist and most imperialist elements of finance capital' (**59**, p. 106). Historians do not, of course, have to be Marxists to argue that Nazism was a type of Fascism. Many would agree with Linz that it was a 'distinctive branch grafted on the fascist tree' (**28**, p. 24). Chronologically, Nazism certainly seems to fit broadly into the context of European Fascism. It shared many of the characteristics of the Italian and other contemporary Fascist movements: extreme nationalism, anti-Semitism and a violent hostility towards communism, socialism and trade unions. Its main support also came from those whose very existence was threatened by the progress of industrialisation and the upheavals of the First World War; and in order to achieve power Nazism, like Italian Fascism, was paradoxically initially dependent on alliances with the industrialists, the great landowners and the generals.

This concept of Nazism as a variant of Fascism is challenged by the 'totalitarian theory', which argues that Nazism in fact was very similar to the Stalinist regime in the Soviet Union. It is true that Nazi Germany superficially appears to have much in common with Stalinist Russia, which was also a single-party state with total government control of the media and a centrally planned economy. Yet, quite apart from the fact that both regimes had different aims, a closer analysis of the way Hitler governed Germany makes any detailed comparison very difficult to make. For instance, there were fundamental differences in the way the Nazi and Soviet Communist parties were organised and functioned.

An influential group of predominantly West German historians, who first began to publish their research in the 1960s (**18, 37**), have rejected both the concept of Fascism and of totalitarianism as being the key to understanding Nazism. In some ways they have returned to the arguments current in the immediate post-war period that Nazism was essentially a product of German history, and have established what has been called a 'new orthodoxy' of interpretation. They argue that in the late nineteenth century German economic, social and political history 'diverged' from the normal patterns of development elsewhere in Europe. They stress that the unprecedentedly rapid rate of industrialisation and urbanisation in Germany, which was accompanied by the rise of organised labour, threatened the traditional life of the peasantry, artisans and lower-middle classes and consequently led to their political radicalisation through the formation of such pressure groups as the Agrarian League or the German League of Artisans, which were rabidly anti-modernist – that is, anti-Semitic, antiliberal and anti-socialist. Not only were these groups exploited politically by the conservative agrarian elite, which still dominated Germany, but they were in their own right a formidable political force which by 1914 broadened the social basis of German conservatism and thus laid the foundations for a popular party of the Right. The 'new orthodoxy' also argues that the constitution that Bismarck created for the Second Reich in 1871 failed in the long term to provide a satisfactory framework in which the Germans could adjust to a modern, pluralist, industrial society. Behind the democratic trappings of universal male suffrage and the Reichstag*, Bismarck ensured that the Reich was ruled by an entrenched Prussian agrarian military elite, which used every means at its disposal to stave off demands for the creation of responsible parliamentary government (**37**).

The social tensions caused by the accelerating speed of the German industrial revolution also encouraged the spread of the *völkisch** philosophy, which by 1914 dominated right-wing thought and was later to form the ideological basis of the Nazi Party. Fritz Stern (**33**) has shown how popular were the *völkisch* writers, de Lagarde, Langbehn and Moeller van der Bruck, and how they preached a nostalgic, anti-modernist ideology which depicted an idyllic Germanic rural society threatened by industrialisation, liberalism and the 'destructive machinations' of the Jews.

There is no doubt that the philosophical, economic and politic&1 roots of National Socialism do lie deep in the nineteenth century. Similarly, it is impossible fully to understand the collapse of German democracy in 1930–33 without reference to the almost permanent state of political crisis that existed in Wilhelmine Germany. On the other hand, all this does not necessarily imply that, because of the course of German history up to 1914, Hitler's triumph in January 1933 was inevitable. Perhaps, as some revisionist historians are now suggesting, Wilhelmine Germany could have evolved peacefully into a more democratic society if war had not broken out in August 1914 (19). The consequences of this disastrous struggle – inflation, the stiff terms of the Versailles Treaty and internal unrest – greatly exacerbated the unresolved conflicts of the Second Reich, which the Weimar Republic (25) inherited in 1919. Little happened in the first five years after the war to inspire confidence in the Republic, and the period of relative stability that followed the Ruhr occupation and the hyper-inflation of 1923 was not long enough to enable it to consolidate itself. By the time the slump hit Germany in 1930 there was no enthusiasm for saving the Republic, and the unprecedented severity of the economic crisis created 'a revolutionary atmosphere in which projects of unusual upheaval could flourish' (34, p. 239).

3

2 Adolf Hitler and the Nazi Party

It could be argued that the history of the Third Reich is synony-mous with Adolf Hitler. After all, his rise to power marked its beginning and his suicide in 1945 its end. Apart from Marxist historians, to whom Hitler is simply a 'puppet of capitalism', probably the majority of historians still seek to explain the Third Reich by reference to Hitler's character, ideas and aims. Indeed, some modern historians such as Hildebrand (59) argue that Nazism was in fact 'Hitlerism' and as such cannot be fitted into the overall category of European Fascism. In the 1960s and 1970s the orthodox view of a virtually all-powerful Hitler began to be challenged by the structuralists, a predominantly West German school of historians, who argued that the study of political leaders and 'great men' needs to be supplemented by a 'structural' analysis of contemporary society (64, 71). In other words, they believe that historians of the Third Reich should concentrate more on explaining how Nazi society worked and on showing that Hitler himself was often a prisoner of forces which he might well have unleashed but which he could not always control. The debate between the structuralists and the more orthodox historians, who still see Hitler as central to the study of the Third Reich, pervades, as will be seen in the chapters below, every aspect of modern research into Nazism. The work of the structuralists has certainly led to a major reassessment of Hitler's role, but on balance it is true to say that few historians would in the final analysis dispute that he still remains a figure of crucial importance in the history of Nazism and the Third Reich.

One of the most dramatic events in contemporary history has been Hitler's metamorphosis from 'the nobody of Vienna into the leader of Greater Germany' (62, p. 12). Nothing in his childhood and years of drifting in Vienna and Munich or in the army during the First World War hinted at the formidable political skills he was to display in building up the Nazi Party. Hitler's unique gift was his ability to match his speeches to the mood of his audiences. Contemporaries bear witness [doc. 1] to how he was able to express what his listeners 'secretly thought and wanted, reinforced their still unsure longings and prejudices, and thereby created for them a deeply satisfying self-awareness' (**64**, p. 24).

Hitler's own precarious existence in Vienna (**1**, **38**), where he absorbed the current anti-Semitic, social Darwinistic and *völkisch* thinking and fanatically identified himself with the Pan-German nationalists, enabled him instinctively to understand the fears of the beleaguered post-war German *Mittelstand**. He himself shared in heightened measure their fear of Bolshevism and their conviction that the Jews were the real cause of all that had gone wrong in Germany since 1918. He acted as a magnet (**64**) for the frightened and the ruined in a post-war Munich that had been particularly hard hit by Germany's economic collapse and had experienced two left-wing coups in 1918–19.

Although Hitler probably only initially envisaged himself as a 'drummer' winning support for a more formidable figure (**56**), he rapidly became the leading politician on the extreme Right in Bavaria and adjusted his ambitions accordingly. He joined the committee of the German Workers' Party in September 1919, which was one of the numerous small *völkisch* parties that had sprung up in Munich after the revolution, and within two years he had not only wrested control from the party's original founders, but had begun to create an organisational structure which subordinated the party to a despotic and charismatic leader (**73**(I)). Within Bavaria the party, which changed its name to the National Socialist German Workers' Party in 1920 (hereafter the Nazi Party), rapidly became the most dynamic force on the Right, especially when its impact was sharpened by the formation of the paramilitary SA* in August 1921. It is a measure of Hitler's standing in right-wing Bavarian circles that he became in 1923 the political leader of the *Kampfbund**, an association of militant groups on the far Right formed to coordinate tactics against the Republic. This step both committed Hitler to a military rather than a political strategy and deprived him of his independence of action because, as plans were drawn up for a putsch*, Kriebel, the military head of the *Kampfbund*, inevitably became the key authority to whom all paramilitary forces, including the SA, were subordinated. The notorious Beer Hall Putsch of 8–9 November 1923 proved a valuable lesson to Hitler on the unreliability of allies and the dangers of gambling everything on a revolt. The success of the putsch depended on cooperation between the *Kampfbund*, the Bavarian *Reichswehr**, and the Conservative authorities in Munich who, however, left Hitler and Kriebel in the lurch at the last moment. Hitler, who had already irretrievably committed himself to action and was under considerable pressure from his own supporters to move, decided to go ahead with the putsch, which ended in disaster on the streets of Munich and in his subsequent imprisonment.

When Hitler came out of prison in December 1924 the Nazi Party had disintegrated, its former members were bitterly divided and the Weimar Republic seemed well on the way to recovery. Nevertheless, over the next four years Hitler rebuilt the party and determined its essential nature until its dissolution in 1945 (**32, 64, 73**(I)). Although Hitler himself was chronically disorganised in his personal life [**doc. 4**], he nevertheless created the organisational base for the party's mushroom growth into a major political party during the depression. Germany was divided into thirty-five *Gaue** or regions, each supervised by a Gauleiter*, below which were the local branches staffed by a cadre of dedicated activists varying in number from district to district. The political party was organised vertically from the party offices in Munich, and each level was subordinated to the one above it. Reflecting the party's new electoral priorities, the *Gaue* were progressively adjusted to dovetail in with the Reichstag* constituencies. This apparently neat vertical pattern was, however, marred by the increasing tendency of the organisations affiliated to the party – the SA*, the Hitler Youth, the Nazi Teachers' Association and so on – to develop their own centralised administration and to see themselves as responsible to the *Führer** alone rather than being mere cogs in the party system. Hitler created a *Führer*-party in which he was the sole source of inspiration and authority. He systematically defeated all attempts to debate policy or share decision-making and promoted an image of himself as a 'myth person' or demi-god who stood far above the mundane arguments and disagreements that frequently occurred within the party. He would only personally intervene if a real crisis occurred, and his day-to-day control of the party increasingly became institutionalised through such party bureaucrats in Munich as Hess, who protected his image without threatening his supreme power.

It is relatively easy to show how Nazism was 'a conglomerate of disparities and contradictions' (**102**, p. 2), but much harder to pinpoint what Hitler's long-term aims were to be once he had gained power. The Nazi Party had possessed a formal programme since 1920 which, besides being nationalistic and anti-Semitic, was also hostile to modern, large-scale capitalism, but Hitler refused to be bound by this and never hesitated to jettison its economic radicalism to win over new supporters. *Mein Kampf** (1), which he wrote in prison, provides the essential key to understanding his first principles, even though it is not a precise blueprint for the future. Page after page bears witness to Hitler's Manichean interpretation of the world as an arena where the supposedly creative forces of the Aryan races clash with the allegedly cunning and evil agents of world Jewry (1). Hitler defined the state in ethnic terms and therefore his whole programme for regenerating Germany depended ultimately on creating a racially pure state which would only then be strong enough to absorb the Germans outside the Reich and acquire *Lebensraum** in eastern Europe.

It was the economic crisis of 1930–33 that turned the Nazi Party into a mass party of protest. Throughout the 1920s German society had continued to disintegrate into a series of interest groups. Hitler showed a genius in appealing to the Germans with what, if it was rationally analysed, was a completely contradictory programme. Nazi propaganda brilliantly built up an image of a party which was youthful, radical, nationalist, both anti-Semitic and anti-Marxist, as well as being sympathetic to small businessmen and peasants without being overtly hostile to the industrialists and *Junkers**. The effectiveness of Nazi propaganda rested partly on the visual or dramatic impact of rallies and meetings, but more importantly on the misleadingly simple but endlessly repeated nature of its slogans, which stressed the Communist danger and the need for a strong, authoritarian government that could offer every class in Germany what it wanted.

Hitler was therefore well placed to exploit the economic crisis. Nevertheless it is quite possible that the new, mass Nazi Party would have melted away again had not the Conservative elites and some of the industrialists seen Brüning's experiment in presidential government as a prelude to the replacement of the Weimar Republic by a more authoritarian government (25). To do this, however, they needed to secure popular backing which only the Nazi Party could provide. Hitler responded to their overtures with caution. He was determined neither to risk an open coup, which would alienate many of his new supporters, nor to enter a coalition in a subordinate position. The very scale of the party's electoral successes after September 1930 and Hitler's ambiguous constitutional tactics subjected the Nazi Party to increasing strains. As the party expanded, friction increased between the party's political

7

organisation and the SA*, which resented the sudden proliferation of party bureaucracy and the stress on electoral success. There were consequently a series of minor but potentially explosive SA strikes and mutinies, the Stennes revolt in April 1931 being one of the most serious. At the same time the number and size of the affiliates increased greatly and they were correspondingly difficult to control. By early 1932 the Nazi Party was rapidly becoming an unwieldy and overblown organisation which was ultimately only kept together by Hitler.

Despite these organisational defects the Nazi Party reached a peak of influence in July 1932. Besides holding 230 seats in the Reichstag* and controlling the government of five of the smaller states the Nazis had also successfully permeated and taken over the Agrarian League (*Landbund*), the artisan associations and several other professional groups. To consolidate the party's successes Gregor Strasser in his capacity as Reich Organisational Leader initiated in 1932 an important series of structural reforms which, in theory at any rate, welded the party for the first and only time into a rational whole. With Hitler's initial agreement he also evolved a long-term programme of action which envisaged at one level Nazi cooperation with the bourgeois parties in the Reichstag, while on a different level the party would continue its successful permeation and take-over of the various interest groups in German society. Hitler, however, rejected this gradual approach to power when he helped to defeat Papen's government in the no-confidence vote in September 1932, thereby committing the party to another election campaign at a time when most political observers agreed that the Nazis had already won all the votes they possibly could. Nevertheless, in taking this decision it is possible that Hitler showed a deeper understanding than Strasser of the real nature of the Nazi Party. The SA's* powerful drive for action would have been difficult to contain had Hitler followed Strasser's plan. At the same time Hitler was also impatient for real power.

The result of the November 1932 elections, in which the Nazis for the first time since 1930 actually lost votes, did not cause Hitler to change his tactics, even though he appeared to be leading the party to a dead end. He stopped Strasser joining Schleicher's cabinet in December 1932, and when he subsequently resigned from the party, Hitler destroyed his organisational reforms, thereby effectively discouraging any coherent planning for the future and causing the party to fragment into often competing sections and interests which could only be held together by mutual loyalty to Hitler. The party was arguably well on its way to 'the rubbish pile of history' (**73** (I), p. 308) when it was rescued, in January 1933, by Papen, who persuaded the President to appoint Hitler Chancellor of a cabinet in which only three out of twelve ministers would be Nazis.

Part Two: The Seizure of Power

3   The Legal Revolution

In 1930 Hitler had publicly declared that 'the constitution only maps out the area of battle, not the goal' (**54**, p. 245). After having been appointed Chancellor on 30 January 1933 by President Hindenburg acting under the terms of Article 48 of the Weimar Constitution, his most immediate aim was to secure complete power, but it was important for him to preserve a camouflage of legality as his repeated emphasis on legal revolution and national unity both won over and fatally confused many who might otherwise have worked against him [**doc. 1**]. In view of the overwhelming non-Nazi majority in the cabinet, Papen's rash boast that within two months 'we will have pushed Hitler so far into a corner that he'll squeak' (**54**, p. 248) seems understandable, but Hitler enjoyed several advantages: two Nazi ministers, Göring and Frick, were responsible respectively for the Ministries of the Interior in Prussia and the Reich; Papen's deposition of the Prussian government in July 1932 had seriously weakened opposition among the other German states to further centralisation and Hitler was able to exploit the state of emergency that had existed since 1930. He was able to invoke Article 48, which theoretically invested emergency powers in the President, to issue a string of emergency decrees. Hitler was also the only politician on the Right to head a mass party. Although the Nazi Party was incapable of governing Germany by itself, it was a powerful negative force held together by loyalty to Hitler and by the prospect of power and the perquisites that go with power (**64**, **73**(II)).

Hitler aimed first to eliminate 'the Reichstag as an effective organ' (**8**(I), p. 126). He rejected the chance of a pact with the Centre Party, which would have secured him a working majority and, despite initial opposition from Hugenberg, who simply wanted to dissolve the Reichstag* without bothering about another election, secured cabinet agreement for going to the country. The Nazis then proceeded to launch a dynamic electoral campaign initiated by a broadcast to the German people on 1 February 1933 (**8**(I), **40**) in which Hitler cleverly played on the nation's longing

10

for unity and recovery. He hid his nihilism, his brutal anti-Semitism and his grandiose plans for expansion into eastern Europe and instead concentrated on the 'appalling inheritance which we are taking over', stressing the total failure of the 'November parties' and the imminent danger of a Communist putsch*. He appealed to the conservative millions of Germany by pledging the new government to 'take under its firm protection Christianity as the basis of our morality and the family as the nucleus of our nation and state' (8(I), p. 132). Hitler's economic plans were vague and woolly, for he was more concerned with creating a delirious atmosphere of national resurgence and branding the 'Marxists' as the national enemy than on committing himself to a sober economic programme.

Even during the election campaign in February Hitler started to lay the foundations of the Nazi dictatorship by presidential decree. On 4 February the government acquired the power to forbid political meetings and to ban newspapers. Two days later the Reich's grip on Prussia was strengthened by the dissolution of the Prussian *Landtag*. Göring now emerged as a key figure in the Nazi takeover of power and began a systematic purge of the Prussian civil service and police. On the 17th the Prussian police, which effectively meant the police in three-fifths of Germany, were ordered actively to support the Nazi Party machine and an extra 50,000 men, predominantly from the SA*, were enrolled as auxiliary police.

An important element in the Nazi campaign was the constant reference to the Communist threat. In fact the Communists, still following instructions from Moscow, were disappointingly docile (**50, Pt 4**), and the Nazis were driven to fabricate proof of an impending Red putsch* by raiding the Communist Party headquarters in Berlin. It was, however, the Reichstag* fire that gave Hitler his best chance to exploit the alleged Red threat. Although the fire was so opportune that contemporaries assumed the Nazis started it, most historians now agree that the half-crazed Dutch Communist, van der Lubbe, was to blame (**50, 51**), although in 1980 a West Berlin court posthumously acquitted him. But it is academic to worry about who actually started the fire for, as Fest has aptly remarked, 'by instantly taking advantage of the fire the Nazis made the deed their own' (**40**, p. 588). On the initiative of Frick, the Reich Minister of the Interior, the formidable 'Decree for the Protection of People and State' was drafted and promulgated on 28 February 1933, empowering the central government not only to arrest individuals at will, censor the post and search private houses, but also to take over the state governments should they refuse to enact 'measures for the restoration of public security'. The decree gave Hitler sufficient power to entrench himself and ensured that his government's fate did not in the final analysis depend on the forthcoming election. It has therefore been described with some justification as 'a kind of *coup d'état*' (**8**(I), p. 142).

Hitler also began to forge the *de facto* coalition with the generals, big business and industry, upon which his second government was unofficially to be based (**103**). On 3 February, at a dinner organised by von Hammerstein, the Commander-in-Chief of the *Reichswehr**, Hitler outlined in full his plans for rearmament and consequently won the grudging recognition that 'at any rate no chancellor has ever expressed himself so warmly in favour of defence' (**80**, p. 291). Hitler's anti-socialism was increasingly appreciated by big business, and thus when he met a group of leading industrialists a little over two weeks later, he was able to win not only their goodwill but also considerable sums for his campaign funds by stressing the anti-democratic and anti-socialist nature of his campaign.

When Germany went to the polls on 5 March 1933, Hitler did not secure the decisive majority he was hoping for. The Nazis won only 43.9 per cent of the votes and could only claim a majority on the strength of their alliance with the Nationalist Party, which was supported by a mere 8 per cent of the electorate. In many Catholic and working-class areas the Nazi Party suffered a decisive defeat and it failed to gain an overall majority in Bavaria, Baden, Württemberg, Hesse and Saxony. Nevertheless, the momentum of the Nazi drive for power was not checked. On the contrary, the election results released a new burst of revolutionary and terrorist activities which won the Nazis the physical control of Germany. While the sheer force of the 'revolution from below' undoubtedly strengthened Hitler's hand and enabled him to neutralise opposition and to force the remaining non-Nazi state governments into resignation between 6 and 20 March, it would be a simplification to argue that Hitler manipulated this explosion at will. To a degree that is hard to determine Hitler had initially to go with the tide of Nazi violence. All over the Reich Nazis seized administrative positions in local government, and there was a growing danger that the German administrative machine would disintegrate in the hands of incompetent Nazi activists. Consequently, in

April the Law for the Re-establishment of the Professional Civil Service hastily confirmed the continued existence of the traditional state bureaucracy even though it was purged of Jews and socialists (**64**).

Hitler was also worried that excessive popular violence would alienate both his coalition partners and the Reich President, and therefore attempted with some success on 10 and 12 March to control his supporters' worst excesses. On 21 March, in a contrived but impressive ceremony at Potsdam, Hitler celebrated the opening of the new Reichstag* in the presence of the Crown Prince and the military establishment of the *ancien régime* and skilfully reawakened memories of the unity of August 1914. Two days later the Reichstag met to consider the Enabling Bill, the aim of which was to legalise the transfer of full legislative and executive powers to the Chancellor for a period of four years. As it entailed a major change in the constitution, the government had to secure a two-thirds majority. Hitler simplified his task by locking up the 81 Communist deputies and winning over the splintered liberal parties, but he still needed the votes of the Centre Party if the bill was to have a secure passage. Against Brüning's advice, the Centre Party decided to support the government, believing mistakenly that it would in time be able to influence Hitler [**doc. 2**].

The debate on the Enabling Bill in the Kroll Opera House took place in the atmosphere of a *coup d'état* (**38**). The square outside was packed with enthusiastic supporters of the Nazis while inside the building SA* and SS* men lined the walls and corridors. Although Hitler went out of his way to stress that the existence of the two houses of parliament (Reichstag* and Reichsrat*), the Presidency, the Christian churches and even the federal states themselves would not be permanently impaired by the bill, he also made it absolutely clear that if the Reichstag did not give him the necessary majority he was 'prepared to go ahead in face of the refusal and the hostilities which will result from that refusal' (**38**, p. 269). This combination of terror and specious pledges won Hitler the required two-thirds majority and the Enabling Bill passed through both houses and duly became law – only the Socialists (SPD*) dared vote against it.

The Enabling Law was of immense propaganda value. Although its constitutional validity is debatable, as it was passed by a Reichsrat* which, 'after the dismemberment of the state governments by coups, unquestionably was not properly constituted' (**54**, p. 250), it maintained the façade of the legal revolution and removed any doubts the civil service or the judiciary had as to the legality of the Nazi take-over. It was this apparent legality that inhibited and confused all but the most clear-sighted opponents of the Nazi regime.

4 The Consolidation of Power

Perhaps the least puzzling aspect of the Third Reich is the ruthless way in which the Nazi movement defeated its enemies. There was, for example, little ambiguity in the way in which the Socialist Party was destroyed or the political parties dissolved. Nazism, as Rauschning observed (61), was primarily a destructive force. The history of the Third Reich becomes more difficult to understand when attempts are made to analyse what positive steps Hitler took to create a new regime to replace what he had destroyed. The Nazi Party did not completely control the Third Reich, but in the final analysis Hitler arguably did. As will be seen later, Hitler replaced the Republic with a chaos of conflicting agencies and ministries in which the party, the traditional state bureaucracy and individual high-ranking Nazis battled with one another to extend their empires (64, 75, 102). Hitler remained in the background as an aloof ultimate authority. Thus Hitler's 'control' of Germany was primarily negative in that real opposition was ruthlessly crushed, whereas a wide range of tolerance was granted to those who sought only to build up their own individual empires whilst publicly vying with their rivals in stressing their complete loyalty to the Führer*.

By the autumn of 1933 Hitler had destroyed what remained of the pluralistic Republic. With the exception of the Presidency, the army and the churches, every organisation was brought under Hitler's ultimate control by the process known as coordination or Gleichschaltung*. His success cannot only be attributed to terror but must also be explained by the perplexing spell he continued to weave over Germany. His rallies, speeches and constant appeals for unity gave him the air of being the leader of an irresistible revolution which, despite its inevitable displays of brutality, was basically a positive force bringing about the spiritual and economic renewal of Germany [doc. 1]. The potential opposition to Hitler was formidable, but it was divided and crippled by fatally under-estimating the dynamism of the Nazi movement. The Nationalist Party, big business, the Reichswehr*, the Vatican, and even the trade unions and SPD* thought, each in its own way, that by appeasing Hitler they could ride out the storm and salvage the essentials necessary for their existence.

Hitler rapidly completed the process of coordinating the states which had already begun before the Enabling Bill was passed. On 31 March their Diets were reconstituted to reflect the ratio of the parties in the Reichstag*, and a week later governors were appointed with full powers to dismiss recalcitrant ministers and to draw up their own legislative programmes. In January 1934, despite Hitler's promises to the contrary, the Diets were finally abolished and all the state governments were firmly subordinated to the Reich government.

Hitler's potentially most formidable opponents were the unions. In 1920 they had defeated the Kapp putsch* by calling a general strike, but by 1933 their members, like most other Germans, were shell-shocked by the slump and the dole queue and in no psychological position to oppose the apparently inevitable Nazi revolution (**49**). The leaders of the socialist unions, which were by far the largest and most powerful in Germany, hoped to salvage at least the essentials of their organisation by assuring Hitler that they would not meddle in politics and would limit themselves merely to protecting the economic and social welfare of their members. On 13 April they even provisionally agreed to the creation of a Nazi *Reichskommissar** for the unions, but any compromise with Hitler was of course impossible. Goebbels outmanoeuvred the union leadership by appealing over its head to the workers. He declared 1 May as a national holiday in honour of labour and invited the workers to participate in the processions and ceremonies which were to mark it. Then on 2 May the SA* and SS* occupied trade-union offices throughout Germany, and both unionised and non-unionised workers were enrolled in the new German Labour Front. Hitler carefully ensured that the Labour Front did not become the genuine voice of even the Nazi workers by handing over responsibility for fixing wages at plant level and for preserving 'industrial peace' to specially created Trustees of Labour who were directly responsible to the Ministry of Labour.

Hitler also moved to coordinate all the various extra-parliamentary associations and private armies that had proliferated on both the Right and the Left before 1933. The left-wing organisations were speedily dissolved, but their right-wing counterparts were integrated into existing Nazi affiliates. The Christian Peasants Association, for example, was merged into the party's Political Agrarian Apparatus, while the *Stahlhelm**, the right-wing ex-soldiers' league, was incorporated into the SA*. The 'Law against the New Formation of Parties' of 14 July confirmed the dissolution of the political parties and made the Nazi Party the only legal party in Germany. Except for the SPD* and the Communists (KPD*), the parties had voluntarily dissolved themselves. The mysterious death of Ernst Oberfohren, the head of the Nationalist Party's Reichstag* delegation, who had dared to criticise Hitler's policies and to question whether his party's coalition with the Nazis should continue, was in the final instance a reminder of what could befall political dissenters of any political colour!

Nazi control of education, the media and the cultural life of the Reich was established with little difficulty. By the spring of 1933 Goebbels, as Minister of Propaganda, controlled broadcasting and adroitly, through a system of internal press conferences and directives, imposed 'a uniformity of news and interpretation' on the papers (**54**, p. 321). In September all 'intellectual workers' were forced to join the Reich Chamber of Culture, which enabled a rigorous check to be kept on their activities. In May the Ministry of the Interior compelled the German states to introduce new syllabuses into the schools and universities. All teachers' and university lecturers' associations were affiliated to the National Socialist Teachers' Organisation. At the universities, gangs of Nazi students terrorised left-wing or free-thinking dons and forced them to resign.

Businessmen and industrialists were more effective in defending their essential interests. The populist or radical wing of the Nazi Party, led by Feder, Otto Wagener and Strasser, campaigned vigorously for the immediate realisation of the original Nazi programme involving the destruction of the department stores and industrial cartels and the subsequent enhancement of small-scale business. As Hitler needed an effective modern industry to stabilise the economy and to rearm Germany, at the end of June 1933, after 'a chaotic interim period' (**102**, p. 129) in which the initiative in economic policies had threatened to pass to Feder and Wagener, economic reality forced Hitler to stop party attacks on big business (**103**). He appointed Schmitt, the managing director of Germany's largest insurance company, to replace Hugenberg as Economics Minister. Industry and business did not, however, entirely escape coordination. In June the employers' associations were welded into the Estate of German Industry, and seven months later the whole of German business was regrouped along functional and territorial lines under the umbrella of the Reich Economic Chamber; but, unlike other victims of coordination, businessmen and industrialists were effectively able to manage their own affairs and keep the more radical members of the Nazi Party out of key positions.

Apart from the *Reichswehr** the only other bodies initially strong enough to bargain with, or even oppose, Hitler were the Lutheran and Roman Catholic Churches. The Concordat signed between the Vatican and the German government on 14 July 1933 appeared to give the Catholic Church substantial advantages which not even the Weimar Republic had offered, and to more than compensate for the dissolution of the Centre Party by securing freedom for the Church to administer its own affairs (**13**). The Concordat only seriously began to be undermined once the Catholic population in the Saar had voted overwhelmingly for their inclusion in the Reich in the plebiscite of 1935 (**23**). It was, however, from the Lutheran Church that Hitler unexpectedly met opposition. Initially there was an attempt to coordinate the Church by setting up a *Reichskirche** under Bishop Otto Müller, an ardent Nazi and former military chaplain, but it was immediately challenged by a strong dissident group, which formed the Confessional Church and in 1934 actually claimed to be the only legitimate Lutheran Church in Germany. In 1935 Hitler was forced to remove Müller and create a new Department of State for Church Affairs, but the Confessional Church managed to survive despite a lack of internal cohesion and considerable persecution (**85, 89**).

5 The Defeat of the Second Revolution

It is a cliché that revolutions devour their children. Both Robespierre and Lenin were compelled to liquidate over-zealous revolutionaries whose opposition threatened their policies. Hitler was not spared this process. The ambiguities and apparent compromises of the 'legal revolution' of 1933, which left the army and big business still intact, were increasingly criticised by the SA* and the populist wing of the party. The Nazi activists had hoped that the seizure of power would entail both 'tangible economic benefits' (73(II), p. 23) and the immediate availability of prestigious new posts, but the party was never to enjoy a monopoly position in the state comparable to that possessed by the Communist Party in Russia, and by July 1933 it was becoming clear that Hitler could not afford to give free rein to its more radical policies. Although there was considerable resentment in the party at the delay in implementing a real Nazi revolution involving the destruction of large-scale capitalism, and the replacement of the *Reichswehr** and the traditional bureaucracy by new, party-dominated structures, only Ernst Röhm possessed a sufficiently strong power base to become an effective critic of, or, in the final resort, a challenge to, Hitler. As the Chief of Staff of the SA he controlled a unique and potentially revolutionary instrument which was a combination of an embryonic people's army and a revolutionary pressure group that terrorised the population into accepting the Nazi seizure of power (49, 69). The SA had never been properly integrated into the Nazi Party. Hitler saw it as a private army strictly subservient to the political arm of the party, whereas the SA leaders saw themselves as latter-day Scharnhorsts laying the foundations for a future people's army.

Once Hitler had declared an end to the 'legal revolution' in July 1933, the SA* increasingly became an 'embarrassing legacy of the years of struggle' (38, p. 286), and was in the process of becoming a mere political auxiliary army whose task was to raise money and to run propaganda activities. Röhm, of course, was unwilling to accept this role and continued to expand the SA until, by the end of 1933, it was a potential army of some two and a half million men. He saw the SA* and SS*, which was still attached to the SA, as the 'incorruptible guarantors' of the completion of a second and much more radical revolution (49). Röhm's thinking on the social, political and economic aspects of the Second Revolution was vague and incoherent. He had considerable sympathy with the more socialist aspects of the Nazi programme (69), but one can only say with certainty that for him the Second Revolution would hinge on turning the SA into a 'huge militia base for a thoroughly rearmed Germany organized along more or less national-bolshevik lines' (73(II), p. 57). It was not so much these incoherent ideas that threatened Hitler but rather Röhm's growing insistence on absorbing the *Reichswehr** and asserting the primacy of the SA over the political wing of the party.

The majority of historians agree that Röhm's elimination was inevitable (40, 64, 69). Although Hitler's whole system of government both encouraged and resulted in rivalry between the various Nazi leaders and their departments, Röhm was in a different category from the other Nazi barons, as he had the means to challenge Hitler and was not dependent upon him. An SA* revolution would have inevitably damaged the prospects of the other party leaders, who were already ensconced in powerful positions and for the most part dependent on the skills of the traditional bureaucracy. Consequently, by the spring of 1934, at the latest, they were ready to goad Hitler into a showdown with the SA (75). Yet it is quite possible that Hitler would have put off a confrontation with Röhm, if in the summer of 1934 the growing rivalry between the SA and the army and, more importantly, the imminent question of the succession to the Presidency which was posed by Hindenburg's ill-health and great age, had not become acute (38, 73(II)).

The continued existence of the *Reichswehr** was essential if Hitler was to embark upon a major rearmament programme and reintroduce conscription [doc. 3]. It can thus be argued that this fact alone made a Hitler–Röhm clash inevitable (40). In all crucial military decisions Hitler favoured the *Reichswehr* (78). In a series of policy statements in 1933 he confirmed that the SA* would be put under the command of the *Reichswehr* and be relegated to supervising the military education of youth groups. In January 1934 Hitler made a more fundamental decision when he consented to the drawing up of plans for the eventual reintroduction of traditional military conscription, thereby finally destroying Röhm's hopes of a people's army (**49**). However, only in retrospect can these decisions be seen as a victory for the *Reichswehr*, because right up to June 1934 there was no guarantee that Röhm would not use the SA to force Hitler to initiate a second revolution (**78**).

By the spring of 1934 the imminent prospect of Hindenburg's death confronted Hitler with the dual necessity of both preventing a second revolution and nipping what could amount to a potential counter-revolution in the bud. In both operations the army's support was the key to success. The 'legal revolution' had left the army and potentially quite strong conservative forces in industry and the civil service still unbroken. There was consequently the possibility that after Hindenburg's death they might unite in the demand for a monarchist restoration, which was arguably the last remaining chance of checking or even toppling Hitler (**49**). However, provided that Hitler could control the SA*, the *Reichswehr** at least would hesitate to support a restoration, as both Blomberg, the Defence Minister, and Fritsch, the new Commander-in-Chief of the Army, as well as a significant number of junior officers, were impressed by Hitler's determination to rearm Germany. It is debatable whether Hitler actually concluded a secret pact with the generals, whereby in exchange for the elimination of Röhm they would back him as Hindenburg's successor (**38, 80**), but it is obvious that both parties had strong reasons for cooperating, and there is indisputable evidence that the *Reichswehr* supplied weapons and lorries to the SS* units which liquidated Röhm at the end of June (**22**).

Although there is some disagreement as to the degree to which Hitler master-minded the purge, it is safe to say that, at the very least, from March 1934 onwards 'he moved erratically and with spells of doubt and indecision towards a show-down with the SA' (**22**, p. 588). Hitler's occasionally flagging resolution was bolstered by those 'advocates of bureaucratic power management' (**73**(II), p. 111), Göring, Himmler and Hess, who were impatient to remove once and for all the dangerous potential of the SA*. The months of May and June were a period of growing tension, even though on 6 June Röhm agreed to relieve it by sending his men on leave for July. Eleven days later, however, Hitler received a sharp reminder from Papen, who informed him in a sensational speech at Marburg University that the longer he delayed in solving the Röhm problem the more likely he was to face growing conservative opposition to his regime. Although Hitler now had little choice but to eliminate not only Röhm but also the leaders of the monarchist movement, he left it to Himmler, Göring, Reichenau and Adolf Wagner, the Gauleiter* of Munich and Bavarian Minister of the Interior, to stage bogus SA revolts in Berlin and Munich, which gave him the excuse to unleash the purge (**40**).

In the 'Night of the Long Knives' on 30 June Röhm and the main SA* leaders and two key monarchists in Papen's office, Bose and Jung, as well as other political enemies of Hitler such as Schleicher and Gregor Strasser, along with an unknown number of lesser figures, were liquidated. Although Hitler's popularity in the nation as a whole probably declined sharply, he was nevertheless able to consolidate his power without difficulty. On the day Hindenburg died (1 August) Hitler combined the offices of Chancellor and President – a step which was confirmed by plebiscite on 19 August.

The populist wing of the Nazi Party was for the time being decisively checked, and both the SA* and the economic radicals had no alternative but to accept Hitler's opportunist interpretation of the Nazi revolution. The SA became a mere propaganda arm of the party, unable to compete with the army. Hitler had indeed defeated Röhm's primitive revolutionary threat, but Germany was now to experience the bewildering yet all-pervading Hitlerian revolution imposed from above, which was not even to spare the army.

Part Three: The Third Reich, 1933–39

6 Party and State

When 'a group of personal failures animated by a desire to destroy liberalism and pluralism in Germany and grouped around a fanatical, charismatic and unstable leader took over the reins of one of the most sophisticated governmental structures in Europe' (**73**(II), p. 17), the consequences were bound to be chaotic and to defy any rational analysis. Despite the veneer of efficiency that so impressed the majority of contemporary observers, in retrospect it is clear that the Third Reich was a Bedlam of rival hierarchies, competing centres of power and ambiguous chains of command (**64, 66, 70, 74, 102**). The Nazi Party failed to dictate policy in the way the Bolshevik Party was able to in Russia, although it did achieve a certain degree of negative control over the state. Thus the traditional civil service retained much of its power and the ambiguous dualism of party and state was never conclusively resolved.

Despite attempts by individual Nazi leaders to develop a coherent overall strategy, Hitler had no immediate blueprint for constructing a specifically Nazi state in 1933. When he became Chancellor he relied on the precedents set by the use of Article 48 to promote the emergency decrees of 28 February and 23 March. The Nazi Party merely took over the existing state and either occupied the key national and local positions or ensured they were in reliable hands (**48, 73**(II)). There was no major purge of the civil service or the diplomatic service and no immediate attempt was made to clarify relations between party and state. However, although no new revolutionary constitutional organs comparable to the Russian soviets were introduced, there were initially some signs of the embryonic growth of the Nazi state. On 29 March 1933 Hitler told his Gauleiters* that 'the work done outside the state organs was decisive', thereby seeming to imply that the party would increasingly take political decisions (**73**(II), p. 44). Despite the emergence of such agencies as Rosenberg's Foreign Affairs Office, which threatened to rival the traditional Foreign Office, and the Nazi Academy of Law, which seemed to herald the nazification of the legal system, the established ministers remained intact and, indeed, were even strengthened when the traditional federal structure of the Reich was abolished in January 1934. As the Nazi Party was only partly able to impose its will on the state, the exact nature of party–state relations defied definition. Walther Sommer, one of the senior officials in Hess's Office of the Deputy *Führer**, fulsomely remarked: 'Only one person, the Führer, knows what the new state will look like after ten years', and Gottfried Neese, the Deputy Leader of the National Association of Civil Servants, noted that 'the mosaic [of party–state relations] is not yet complete, but the observer feels intuitively that a planned concept will be realised in the future' (**73**(II), p. 169). In a series of paradoxical statements Hitler attempted to define party–state relations. In July 1933 he observed that the 'party had now become the state' and that all power lay with the Reich government (**8**(I), p. 171). Then, three months later, at the Nuremberg rally, the party was given the task of both educating the people and of assimilating a new political elite, but he again cryptically observed that 'those problems which can be solved by the state will be solved by the state, but what the state is inherently unable to solve will be solved by the movement' (**8**(II), p. 236). By the 'Law to Ensure the Unity of Party and State' of 1 December 1933 the party was made a corporation under public law and declared to be 'the bearer of the concept of the German state' and to be 'inseparably linked with the state' (**8**(II), p. 231), but there was no real attempt to define what this meant in constitutional terms.

The most easily identifiable function of the party was its task of controlling and educating the masses. Through such affiliated organisations as the SA*, the Hitler Youth and the German Labour Front the population was both controlled and brainwashed. Even though the decision to limit the party to an elite of 10 per cent was taken in 1939, the great majority of the population was associated with the party through the affiliates. The party's role as an assimilator of the elite was, however, less successful. Despite elaborate attempts to create elite training schools, the men who graduated from these 'were the opposite of sophisticated' (**73**(II), p. 191), and it was also clear that a purely party career failed to attract applicants of high calibre. University graduates, even if they now joined the party, continued to enter the traditional civil and diplomatic services (**102**).

The party's other main task was to supervise rather than actually run the state. The party's grip on the state was stronger in theory than in practice, but it was able to block any legislation or executive regulations of which it disapproved, provided it could make up its collective mind. Hess, as Deputy *Führer**, was empowered to participate both in drafting legislation and in appointing officials. In effect, the party practised a negative control over the state and civil service. Provided it had Hitler's backing it could force out of office or block the appointment of any candidate who did not enjoy its confidence. 'The Law for the Re-establishment of the Professional Civil Service' of April 1933 purged the service of Jews and known opponents of the regime, while the Civil Service Act of 1937, which made officials directly responsible to Hitler as 'executors' of the Nazi state, ensured that promotion within the service was entirely dependent on a good political record. Finally, in February 1939, party membership became an essential condition for any new entrant to the service (**102**).

One of the most paradoxical aspects of the Third Reich was the failure of the party to dictate consistently to the state. Individual ministers, some of whom were even Nazis, like Frick at the Ministry of the Interior, vigorously defended their departments from party interference. Provided that the expressed will of the *Führer** was not flouted it was frequently possible to check the growth of party influence by a series of procedural wrangles, and it has been argued by Orlow that civil servants learned to see 'the party as a rival but not necessarily as an invincible one' (**73**(II), p. 135).

The traditional ministries were not, however, immune from the more insidious consequences of the Nazi revolution. It was part of Hitler's policy to encourage the growth of a bewildering number of *ad hoc* agencies, whilst still leaving the traditional institutions intact. Consequently, 'new institutions grew, flourished or died, spawned mutations, struggled for survival and thrust their offshoots under the very doors of the established ministries' (**102**, p. 209). The Foreign Office was first threatened by Rosenberg's Foreign Affairs Office and then more seriously undermined by Ribbentrop's bureau which for a time became the 'incubator of Nazi foreign policy' (**102**, p. 212).[1] Even the army was unable to preserve its original position of being a 'state within a state'. In the aftermath of the Röhm putsch* Blomberg committed the army to taking a personal oath of loyalty to Hitler. In February 1938 its independence was irreparably damaged when Hitler, exploiting

---

[1]When Ribbentrop became Foreign Minister in 1938 he embarked upon a thorough nazification of the diplomatic service, which was only halted by the war (**129**).

the Officer Corps' reaction to Blomberg's 'mésalliance' with a former callgirl and the allegations that Fritsch, the Commander-in-Chief of the Army, was a homosexual, abolished the post of War Minister and took over the command of the armed forces himself. He also retired sixteen high-ranking officers who represented a potential threat to him (**78, 79, 80**).

At regional level the rivalry between the state and the party was equally evident. The ten Reich governors, who were in most cases Gauleiters*, were supposed to ensure that party policies were implemented, but in practice they were frequently outwitted by the professional skills of the local *Regierungspräsidenten** in Prussia or the *Ministerpräsidenten** in the other states, who could usually rely on the backing of the Reich Ministry of the Interior. It was, however, at district and local level that the party exercised most influence. The Gauleiters had built up strong grass-roots support, and in many areas the Nazis dominated the local town councils. The Reich Local Government Law of 30 January 1935 provided for the participation of the Nazi Party in the appointment and dismissal of mayors and local councillors (**8(II)**).

Although the Nazi Party was undoubtedly one of the key power blocs in the Third Reich (**60**), it was too divided and too lacking in genuine administrative ability to create a proper Nazi state. The party was not a tight, well-integrated group, but a movement which was often paralysed by dissensions and mutual distrust. The Nazi leaders were more intent on building up their own power than on developing a consensus for future action. Consequently only in a few areas before 1939 could the party claim to have decisively imposed its will on the state. Arguably its greatest success was to force the state to accept the Nuremberg race laws (see page 46) which made the party's racial policy legally binding even though these laws were in fact seen as victory for the moderates over the radicals (**73(II)**).

It is quite probable that without the steadying effect of Himmler Hitler's divided state might well have collapsed as a result of its own internal contradictions. Himmler underpinned the Third Reich with the Gestapo* and the SS* (**65, 67, 68, 75, 76**). The SS had been formed in 1925, but it only began to become important when Himmler, who has been characterised as a 'shrewd practitioner of power with an eye to the main chance' (**22**, p. 598), took it over in 1929. Under Himmler the SS became all that the SA* was not: a loyal, highly disciplined elite. Its power was greatly increased when it was made responsible for the party's intelligence and espionage section in 1932. By June 1934 Himmler virtually controlled the local police forces in the states, including the Gestapo in Prussia. As a reward for its loyalty the SS was made independent of the SA in July 1934, and two years later Himmler's appointment as Chief of the German Police confirmed his dual command over the SS and the police. Himmler then went on to create an organisation which 'potentially superseded the state' (102, p. 240) and perhaps even the party as well. By 1941 the 'SS* state' was a reality. In Schoenbaum's words: 'in one form or another the SS made foreign policy, military policy and agricultural policy. It administered occupied territories as a kind of self-contained Ministry of the Interior and maintained itself economically with autonomous enterprises' (102, p. 240). Most of these developments were already foreshadowed before the war. The *Waffen* SS rapidly developed into an embryonic army, even though it did not begin to challenge the power of the *Wehrmacht** until the last two years of the war (75). After the Röhm putsch* responsibility for administering the concentration camps was transferred from the SA* to the SS, and the notorious Death's Head Units (*Totenkopfverbände*) were created to police them. It was, however, in Austria and the Sudetenland that the SS state expanded most rapidly. After the *Anschluss** in 1938 Himmler was given a free hand to round up all potential dissidents and to incarcerate them in Mauthausen concentration camp. Eichmann, the chief of the Gestapo's Jewish Office, was installed in Vienna as the director of the Jewish Emigration Bureau. He was so successful in carrying out a brutal policy of forced emigration that Göring set up the Reich Central Office for Jewish Emigration under Heydrich, the chief of the Security Police, to pursue similar policies in Germany and the occupied territories of the Sudetenland and Bohemia (8(II)). By the winter of 1939–40 he was organising forced deportations of Jews to Poland, and by 1941 he was planning, through the Office for Jewish Emigration, the extermination of Europe's Jewry. The basis of SS power in the occupied territories was laid when in October 1939 Himmler was appointed Plenipotentiary for resettlement questions in occupied Europe, and its monopoly in racial matters was confirmed when Himmler became, a few weeks earlier, '*Reichskommissar* for the strengthening of the German race'. Neither did Himmler neglect to tap any form of profit which could help render the SS independent of both party and state. In the winter of 1938–39 two companies were formed to exploit economically the work of the inmates of Sachsenhausen, Dachau and Buchenwald.

The only arbiter between the mass of conflicting agencies which composed the Third Reich was Hitler himself (**54**). In theory Hitler was all-powerful. He combined in his position as *Führer** 'the functions of supreme legislator, supreme administrator and supreme judge' and was also 'the leader of the Party, the Army and the People' (**60**, p. 74). The very lack of a recognised constitution gave Hitler greater power than ever Napoleon, Mussolini or even perhaps Stalin enjoyed, as there was no effective institution which could in an emergency gain the strength to check him (**38**). The cabinet met only rarely after 1934, the Reichstag* was reduced to the role of a rubber stamp, and the Presidency was abolished. Yet, strangely, Hitler did not play a prominent part in day-to-day government. Petersen has described him as a 'remote umpire handing down decisions from on high' (**74**, p. 4) when his subordinates could not agree among themselves, and has been surprised by the paucity of documents that bear his signature. Hitler hated paper work and delegated as much of it as possible to his subordinates. He disliked the mental effort required to come to a decision and usually preferred to let events take their course rather than intervene [**doc. 4**].

While there is a consensus among historians that the administration of the Third Reich was a chaotic system of rival and overlapping areas of responsibility (**164**), opinions differ sharply on the reasons for this. The intentionalists, or those who believe that Hitler's aims or intentions should be taken seriously (**49**, **59**), stress that Hitler deliberately encouraged rivalry among his supporters to safeguard his own position, while the structuralists (see page 4) (**64**, **71**) argue that the administrative chaos was an inevitable consequence of Hitler's unstable, charismatic rule. Hitler's wishes, in domestic policy at any rate, were often little more than vague declarations of intent or even propaganda and as such were almost impossible to translate precisely into clear laws and unambiguous directives.

This chaos at the heart of the Nazi regime can give an impression of weakness. Neumann, writing as far back as 1942, was convinced that Hitler's policies were compromises dictated by the big four power blocks in the Third Reich: the army, the party, the bureaucracy and big business. He called the Third Reich a Behemoth or 'a nonstate, a chaos, a situation of lawlessness, disorder and anarchy' (**60**, p. 375). Hans Mommsen has come to the conclusion that Hitler was 'reluctant to take decisions, often uncertain, concerned only to maintain his own prestige and personal authority, and strongly subject to the influence of his environment – in fact, in many ways, a weak dictator' (**59**, p. 137), while David Irving has provocatively described Hitler as 'probably the weakest leader Germany has known this century' (**118**, Intro.). Was Hitler really so weak? There is little evidence that Hitler wanted to be involved in the day-to-day domestic policy. Indeed, his charismatic system depended on his very aloofness from such matters. In some senses he could be compared to a feudal monarch, who mediated between the claims of his rival barons, all of whom had sworn complete loyalty to him (**74, 164**). It is easy to exaggerate Hitler's powers and see him as omnipotent. As with all politicians there were very definite limits to his powers. He was, for instance, particularly subject to pressure from the party rank and file on his policies for solving the Jewish 'problem', and there were certain intractable economic difficulties which defied easy solutions. Yet Hitler was no weak dictator. In a negative sense he did control Germany, in that he had broken most potential centres of opposition to his regime. In those areas of policy in which he was interested, particularly foreign policy and rearmament (see Chapters 7, 10 and 11), he was also able effectively – at least in the short term – to implement his policies. Perhaps his weakness, if such it can be described, depended rather on the inherent instability of the regime he had created (**71**).

7 The Economy

Hitler's economic policy was frequently a series of compromises between contradictory and even hostile forces. He was committed to save the *Mittelstand**and the peasants from economic extinction and at the same time to revive the fortunes of big business; he wished to rearm Germany rapidly and develop a self-sufficient economy, yet he could not politically afford to introduce rationing or sacrifice the standard of living of the working classes; he was prepared to reflate the economy, but dared not completely abandon Brüning's rigid deflationary policy. Despite his ambitious pledges to create employment and to solve the agrarian problem, he had no coherent economic policy in January 1933.

Hitler's first preoccupation as Chancellor was to win the March election and to break any potential opposition. It was not until June 1933 that the Law to Reduce Unemployment was enacted, which applied on a far greater scale many of the tools used by Papen and Schleicher, who had attempted to channel government spending into creating employment while rigorously controlling prices and wages (**88**). As Klein has pointed out, 'the Nazis did not change this basic strategy; they only attempted to make it more effective' (**92**, p. 6). Reichsmarks (RM) were poured into public works, or granted as subsidies for private construction or the renovation of dilapidated buildings (**97**). Increased industrial activity was also encouraged by a whole series of schemes involving income-tax rebates and loans. A separate law initiated a large-scale plan for the construction of 7,000 kilometres of motorway, which, besides appealing to the national imagination and providing employment directly, also stimulated subsidiary industries. There is no doubt that these measures, combined with the opportune upturn in the trade cycle and the absorption of nearly a million unemployed youths by the Labour Service and Emergency Relief Schemes, helped Hitler to bring unemployment down to two and a half million by the middle of 1934 [**doc. 5**]. Relatively large-scale rearmament and the expansion of the chemical and steel industries then enabled Hitler practically to eliminate unemployment by the spring of 1939.

The urgency of the unemployment problem was only rivalled by the plight of the peasantry, who made up 29 per cent of the working population. They were caught between the 'scissors' movement of high prices for industrial goods and low prices for agricultural produce, and many of them were consequently bankrupted (**87**). As immediate measures, Hugenberg, who was also responsible for agriculture until his resignation in June 1933, placed a moratorium on peasants' debts until the end of October 1933, increased tariffs on selected imported foodstuffs, and attempted to assist dairy farmers by ordering the compulsory addition of butter to margarine. In September his successor, Darré, radically reorganised agriculture by setting up the Reich Food Estate and introducing the Reich Entailed Farm Law. The Reich Food Estate was an independent corporate body which was responsible for all aspects of food production, and all farmers, farm cooperatives, agricultural wholesale dealers, and so on were compelled to join it. Through a series of marketing and supervisory boards it controlled crop prices and its staff office was entrusted with the future planning of German agriculture (**55, 87**).

The Reich Entailed Farm Law of 29 September 1933, which sought to retain 'the peasantry as the blood-spring of the German nation', was one of the few pieces of Nazi legislation that was inspired by ideology rather than pragmatism (**102**). It aimed to give the peasantry security of tenure by ruling that farms between 7.5 and 10 hectares were both indivisible and inalienable. The farms were to remain the permanent property of the original peasant owners and consequently could not even be offered as a collateral against a loan. Although the law only applied to about 35 per cent of the agricultural land in Germany, it was a radically conservative measure which fixed the German peasantry 'like a fly in amber at the current stage of its development' (**87**, p. 69). It hindered the development of large-scale modern farming units and thus militated against achieving the very self-sufficiency for which Darré was aiming.

No similar package was devoted to the *Mittelstand**, although initially Hitler could not avoid making some concessions in their direction. In May 1933, for example, the Law for the Protection of the Retail Trade forbade any extension of the much-hated department stores, and two months later further ordinances prohibited them from offering a whole range of services such as baking, hair-cutting and shoe-repairing which now became the monopoly of the small corner shop. Yet significantly the government could not afford to close down the department stores, and in July 1933 it invested over 14 million RM in the Jewish-owned Hertie stores in a successful attempt to prevent their collapse, which would then have thrown thousands out of work (**102**).

Hitler dared not implement the radical *Mittelstand** socialism of the party programme, as he needed the expertise of big business to plan rearmament, to help bring down unemployment, and simultaneously to avoid a financial crash. In June 1933 the 'fighting organizations of the industrial middle classes' were dissolved and their members absorbed into the newly created Estate for Handicraft and Trade, which in its turn was reduced by Schacht, when he became Economics Minister, 'to the status of a mere organization under the control of big business' (**103**, p. 146). In open contradiction to the original Nazi programme [**doc. 1**], the years 1933–36 saw the steady growth of cartels and the influence of big business over the economy – between July 1933 and December 1936, for example, over 1,600 new cartel arrangements were signed (**103**).

Hitler's main priority was to rearm Germany as quickly as possible (**98, 99**). He thus needed in the short term both to save foreign exchange to pay for imported raw materials and to raise the necessary money within Germany to finance rearmament. On 16 May 1933 Hitler prepared the way for a more flexible policy by replacing, as President of the *Reichsbank**, the orthodox financier Luther by Schacht, whose first task was to control the outflow of foreign exchange. In June 1933 he declared a public transfer moratorium on German debts incurred to foreign creditors before July 1931. These debts were now to be paid only in *Reichsmarks,* although for the time being repayments in foreign currencies of the loans which had been raised abroad under the Dawes and Young Plans continued, but in 1934 they too were stopped. Hitler was fortunate that Germany had been virtually freed from the encumbrance of reparation payments at the Lausanne Conference in 1932.

Schacht applied his financial genius to expanding schemes for deficit financing which had only been tentatively experimented with by his predecessors. He introduced new methods for financing rearmament. Government procurement agencies paid industries awarded with military contracts credit notes, or 'Mefo bills', which were issued by a 'dummy organisation' (**103**) of four large private companies and two government ministries disguised as the *Metall-Forschungs AG*[1] (Metal Research Co.), the debts of

The Economy

which were underwritten by the government (110). The
Reichsbank* was ready to exchange Mefo bills for cash, thereby
ensuring the prompt payment of industry, but as they were valid
for a period up to five years the government also tapped a considerable amount of money that was lying idle by offering them,
rather as if they were bonds, at 4 per cent per annum on the
money market as an investment and by compelling both commercial and private savings banks to invest 30 per cent of their deposits
in them.
  The pace of German rearmament was bedevilled by recurring
balance of payments crises. Work creation projects, rearmament,
as well as increased consumer demand, which was a consequence
of Hitler's success in cutting unemployment, resulted in a steep
rise in imports. At the same time Germany found it particularly
hard to increase its exports, as Schacht refused to devalue the
Reichsmark and most other countries had raised their tariffs. The
only long-term solutions were either the creation of a fully self-
sufficient economy or the absolute insistence on the priority of
imports for the armament industries by rationing food and
consumer goods. Hitler himself realised that complete autarky was
impossible within the existing frontiers of the Reich [docs 12, 13],
but shied off imposing a rigid war socialism in peacetime.
  The first major balance of payments crisis blew up in June 1934
and forced the Reichsbank* to impose even stricter limits on the
allocation of foreign exchange (103). The army, fearful for its
rearmament programme, and big business, highly critical of
Schmitt, the Economics Minister, exploited Hitler's vulnerability at
the time of the Röhm putsch* and successfully demanded
Schmitt's replacement by Schacht. Schmitt had made enemies
both by attacking the cartels and by threatening, through
advocating an increase in the purchasing power of the workers, to
unleash a full-scale consumer boom, which would have increased
imports and diverted scarce raw materials away from rearmament
(8(II)). Schacht was given full dictatorial powers in the economic
sphere, and in September 1934 he introduced the New Plan which
set up the necessary controls for the government regulation of
imports and currency exchange. Schacht also saved vital foreign
exchange by negotiating a series of bilateral trade agreements,
mainly with the Balkan and South American states. German
purchases in these countries were paid for in German currency

[1]Hence Me–fo.

33

which could only then be used to buy German goods or to invest in the construction of plants which would later produce goods required for the German economy. Schacht was, however, fundamentally an orthodox financier. In 1934, for example, he had firmly told Hitler that Germany should never buy any more than it could pay for (15). In 1935 he tried to block Darré's emergency request to import large quantities of butter, vegetable oil and fodder, arguing instead that rationing should be introduced, but with Hitler's consent he was overruled by Göring, who feared the public's reaction to rationing. In December 1935 Schacht therefore informed Blomberg that there was now not enough currency to pay for the doubling of copper imports. Schacht argued that the only way to pay for rearmament was to increase the volume of exports – a solution which met with support from commerce and the export-orientated coal, iron and steel industries (22, 99, 100).

Hitler was not prepared at this stage to allow orthodox economic thinking to slow down the rearmament programme. In April 1936 he began to bypass Schacht by appointing Göring Commissioner of Raw Materials and Currency, and then in August, in a memorandum which is 'one of the basic documents of the Third Reich'(8(II), p. 280) [doc. 6], he introduced the Four Year Plan, for the implementation of which Göring was again made responsible. Its ostensible aim was to make Germany as independent as possible of both industrial and agricultural imports, either by increasing production or by inventing substitutes. Within four years both the German economy and army were to be ready for war (22, 99, 100). Over the next few years large plants were built for the production of synthetic rubber and oil and the massive Hermann Göring Steelworks was erected at Watenstedt-Salzgitter to exploit the low-grade ores there. To prevent the economy from overheating, tighter controls of prices, wages and labour were introduced. However, despite impressive achievements, the Four Year Plan failed decisively in meeting production targets in synthetic fuel and rubber, fats and light metals, and consequently the shortage of foreign exchange continued to be a problem.

Contemporaries bombarded by Nazi propaganda and impressed by the imposing military parades in Berlin were convinced that Hitler had completely subordinated the economy to the demands of total war. But in 1959 Klein challenged this orthodox view and argued persuasively that the 'scale of Germany's economic mobilization for war was quite modest' and pointed out that the production of consumer goods increased by over 30 per cent between 1936 and 1939 (**92**, p. 78). Klein's interpretation was modified a few years later by further research (**84**, **96**), which showed that while there was no total war economy up to 1942, nevertheless by 1938 17 per cent of Germany's gross national product was spent on rearmament, which is a sum far greater than any other European power was spending on armaments [**doc. 19**]. On the basis of these figures many historians (**8**(II), **94**, **96**) have argued that Hitler was offering the Germans both guns and butter. More recently Richard Overy in two seminal articles (**98**, **99**) has further challenged Klein's conclusions and shown that the Four Year Plan really was 'a decisive step towards preparing Germany for total mobilization' (**99**, p. 104), which also severely cut investment in the consumer industries. It provided the economic substructure for the later expansion of the armaments industries. Overall, according to Overy, 'consumption as a share of national income declined from 71 per cent in 1928 to 58 per cent in 1938' (**99**, p. 111). These figures certainly suggest that Hitler was planning for war. Initially perhaps he was thinking of only limited *Blitzkrieg**, but ultimately the logic of his rearmament programme pointed in the direction of a major war.

Like most Nazi organisations the administration of the Four Year Plan was impeded by bureaucratic inefficiencies and internal rivalries. Nevertheless, it did enable Hitler to strengthen his hold on the economy, which was arguably one of the Plan's aims (**96**). To administer the Plan Göring set up six offices with special responsibilities for the production and distribution of raw materials, the labour force, agriculture, price control and foreign exchange, which inevitably undermined the powers of the ministries traditionally concerned with the economy (**8**(II)). It is thus not surprising that Schacht's influence rapidly declined. He resigned as minister in November 1937 and was dismissed from the *Reichsbank** in January 1939.

Robert Brady, writing in 1937, described the Nazi regime in orthodox Marxist terms, as the dictatorship of monopoly capitalism (**55**). Up to June 1934 big business certainly appeared to exert considerable influence over the regime, as the defeat of the Nazi populists and the appointment of Schacht seemed to show, but it never dominated the state. It arguably became a partner of the state and army in rearmament, but as Schweitzer has pointed out, the price it had to pay for the profits of this partnership was 'a fairly strict adherence to the market regulations imposed by the state' (**103**). The introduction of the Four Year Plan emphasised that capitalism could only continue to thrive in Germany provided it was ready to subordinate itself to the Nazi government. The chemical industry welcomed the Plan and subsequently prospered, whereas the steel industry, which had been more critical, found itself confronted with a rival giant in the state-owned Hermann Göring Steelworks, the expansion of which was hereafter achieved at the expense of the private sector. Hitler had no intention of expropriating private industry as long as it was useful to him. Indeed, whilst the Four Year Plan enormously increased the potential of the state, it also paradoxically strengthened the tendencies towards the concentration of monopoly power by such large firms as I. G. Farben (**22**). Even state-owned plants like the Hermann Göring Steelworks were organised along traditional capitalist lines and raised capital by selling some of their shares on the open market. Big business remained a partner of the Nazi regime, but as both Guillebaud (**88**) and Neumann (**60**) perceived, it was a partnership that could be terminated by the Nazi Party in the event of a clash of interests.

8 Was there a Nazi Social Revolution?

Nazi ideology, with its stress on the peasant and the artisan and the role of women within the the family, implied that a Nazi social revolution would be primarily a *völkisch** counter-revolution aimed at unscrambling the contemporary pluralist and industrial state. Not surprisingly, some contemporary observers believed that this is exactly what happened (**163**).

However, some 30 years later two important studies by Dahrendorf and Schoenbaum (**86, 102**) came to the conclusion that the Nazi regime triggered a more modern social revolution, which dragged Germany into the twentieth century. Both argued that the Nazi concept of a people's community allied with full employment really did create a more flexible and classless society. Schoenbaum advanced the paradoxical thesis that Hitler presided over a 'double revolution...of means and ends' (**102**, Intro.). By this he meant that on the one hand there was an ideological revolution hostile to the industrial society, but on the other hand, in order to destroy that modern industrial world, Germany had in effect to wage war against it, and this meant rearmament in depth. Thus in fact Hitler had to let the very industrial revolution which he hated make further inroads into traditional German pre-industrial life-patterns. Other historians have further elaborated on Schoenbaum's thesis. Henry Turner, for instance, has argued that Hitler's intended conquest of *Lebensraum** on which he hoped to settle Germany's surplus population would eventually have made possible the de-urbanising and de-industrialisation of Germany. Nevertheless, the paradox remained that these conquests could only be achieved by 'a vast industrial war' (**164**, p. 137). More recently two German historians, Abelshauser and Faust, have put forward a less paradoxical interpretation of the Nazi social revolution. They argue that Nazism played a key role in the modernisation of Germany. It anticipated Keynesian economics by creating full employment, with all the potential for social mobility that this entailed, and by both destroying the trade unions and simultaneously controlling the employers it decisively changed the structure of German society (**164**).

Although the industrial realities of a modern state and the decision to rearm in practice significantly modified the nature of the Nazi social revolution and prevented the realisation of many of its aims, in the more rarefied air of the classroom and the lecture hall a generation was exposed to the contradictory absurdities of the Nazi philosophy (8(II), 55, 83, 89). The traditional structure of the German educational system remained unchanged, even though it was put under the centralised control of the new Reich education minister in May 1934, but the syllabuses were radically revised in the light of Nazi racial, political and social prejudices [doc. 8]. Special emphasis was placed in the school curriculum on History, Biology and German as the three subjects which were particularly effective vehicles for Nazi propaganda. A key to the new priorities was given by Hitler's observation that 'the racial state must build upon its entire educational work ... not on the pumping in of empty knowledge but on the development of healthy bodies. Only in the second place comes the training of mental facilties' (55, p. 107). Consequently, sport became a major subject, and, in Grünberger's words, 'games masters advanced from the periphery of the teaching body almost to the very centre' (89, p. 365). There was also a marked reduction in the number of girls in the grammar schools (*Gymnasien*), and those who remained were encouraged to specialise in domestic science or languages.

The universities did not outwardly change, but their courses, particularly in German and History, were brought into harmony with Nazi prejudices. Even the apparently apolitical science of Physics could become metamorphosed into 'German Physics', which, amongst other things, entailed the root and branch rejection of Einstein's 'Jewish' Theory of Relativity (89). As in secondary education, students were compelled to join in organised games run by the National Socialist Students' Association. Initially the number of women students declined, but full employment and the economic demands of the Four Year Plan pushed their number up, contrary to all earlier statements by the Nazi ideologues, to a record 20 per cent of the whole student population (106, 107).

The potentially most radical educational innovation introduced by the Nazis was the creation of a small number of special schools and institutions which were entrusted with the task of producing the future elite of Germany, the *Napola* (National Political Educational Establishments), the Adolf Hitler Schools and the pseudo-medieval *Ordensburgen** (89). Their task was to toughen or indeed to barbarise the cream of German youth in preparation for its future tasks and responsibilities, but in fact they signally failed to produce a new elite, although their intake was more socially mixed than the traditional grammar schools and universities.

Whilst few chances were missed to brainwash the mass of school-children, the main responsibility for carrying out Hitler's exhortation, 'Be hard, German youth, and make yourselves hard' (3(1), p. 547), was borne by the Nazi youth movements, membership of which became compulsory in December 1936. From the age of ten to fourteen boys joined the *Jungvolk** and then for the next four years the Hitler Youth itself, where they were subjected to the familiar mixture of sport, war games and propaganda. There was a parallel organisation for girls in the *Jungmädel** and the German Girls League where, however, there was greater stress on teaching traditional female domestic skills. Hitler boasted that the Nazi movement had 'sown seeds that have sunk deep' (3(1), p. 616), but it seems that as least as many adolescents were bored by the tedium of drill and often badly organised games as were fired by patriotic enthusiasm (8(II), 89).

Outside the classroom and the make-believe of Hitler Youth manoeuvres Nazi dogma clashed painfully with economic reality. Nothing illustrates this more clearly than the Nazis' failure to stop the accelerated urbanisation and industrialisation of Germany, despite the fact that the peasant was seen as the backbone of society. It is not true to say that the Nazis were cynical about their support for the peasantry, which together with anti-Semitism has been described as 'one of the few consistent premises of Nazi life' (102, p. 161). It is rather that they tried unsuccessfully to combine rearmament with the preservation of a pre-industrial peasant class.

In addition to the Reich Entailed Farm Law the Nazi government attempted to protect the peasantry in a number of ways. The Reich Food Estate took considerable pains to restore the peasants' self-confidence by reviving what was in most cases defunct peasant folklore and impressing on them at every opportunity their role as 'responsible carriers of German society renewing its strength from blood and soil' (87, p. 212). The regime also attempted to stem the migration from the countryside to the towns. During the period 1929–34 migration had all but died out as a result of the slump, but as soon as the economy began to expand it resumed its rapid tempo. In May 1934 labour exchanges were authorised to stop land workers accepting jobs in industry and errant peasants were liable, like escaped slaves, to be returned to their farms, although in practice this rarely happened. Legislation was in fact powerless to prevent what amounted to a mass exodus from the countryside.

The rural population voted with its feet against poverty, poor housing and the back-breaking nature of unmechanised farm work. Consequently the pace of urbanisation quickened and Germany increasingly exhibited all the characteristics of an advanced industrial society.

The Nazis were more successful in their attempts to curtail female emancipation and limit women to their primary task of childbearing (**89, 91, 95, 107**). Nazi attitudes towards women were tempered by a mixture of paternalism and male resentment at the liberated and allegedly promiscuous *Berlinerin* of the Weimar period (**22**) [**doc. 7**]. Before 1929 labour trends indicated that female labour in industry, the professions and commerce would rapidly increase, but the depression interrupted this pattern and severely restricted the opportunities open to women. Hitler consequently exploited this to drive or cajole as many women as he could back into the home. Professional women were hardest hit by his measures. Soon after the seizure of power married women in the higher ranks of the civil service and in medicine were dismissed, and in 1936 the higher legal posts were completely barred to women, who were also categorically excluded from playing any part in politics. It was only in those sections of the party's organisation which dealt exclusively with women that they could enjoy what Mason has called a certain degree of 'surrogate emancipation' (**95**, p. 101).

The Nazis in no way attempted to halt the employment of some four million women on the land or in their husbands' businesses, but they did try to ease women out of industry and commerce by making motherhood an attractive financial proposition through a series of grants, loans, tax-relief schemes and the introduction of family allowances. One scheme, which was perhaps the most subtle example of social engineering in the Third Reich, involved interest-free loans to newly married couples provided the wives withdrew from the labour market. The significant increase in the German birth-rate between 1933 and 1939 [**doc. 9**] is usually attributed to Hitler's financial inducements, although the discouragement of birth-control methods and the crack-down on back-street abortionists may well have played an equally important role. Mason, with the healthy scepticism of the historian, wonders whether the rise in the population was more a result of the end of the depression than a positive response to Hitler's financial bribes, and tentatively suggests that 'the massive rhetorical institutional and financial encouragement of motherhood had little impact on people's behaviour' (**95**, p. 103).

Overall the Nazis failed in their campaign to confine women to the home, although initially their policy appeared successful as it coincided with the withdrawal of female labour as a consequence of the slump. They could make little headway in the long term against the growing trend of employing young adult women in the consumer goods industries simply because employers found them cheaper than men. By 1937, at a time of growing labour scarcity, women were also recruited to work in many of the new plants set up under the Four Year Plan. Thus once again the Nazi government 'found itself in head-on collision with a long-term process of social and economic change' (**95**, p. 93) and in 1937 was compelled to relax its ruling that only unemployed married women were eligible for the marriage loan.

Hitler's most controversial claim was that his government had 'broken with a world of prejudices' [**doc. 10**] and created a genuine people's community. To evaluate this assertion it is necessary to assess the fate of the urban working class in the Third Reich. Although Nazism had drawn most of its votes from the peasantry and the *Mittelstand** in 1933, it nevertheless could not afford to alienate the proletariat. Thus Hitler justified the dissolution of the trade unions and the political parties of the Left by claiming paradoxically that he had liberated the workers from their bureaucratic and corrupt Marxist leaders and given them a more respected place in society (**89, 94, 102**). Bereft of union protection, the workers were forced to join the Labour Front, to have their wages fixed by the Trustees of Labour and to witness the enhancement of the authority of their employers, who now were officially called 'plant leaders'. In all factories where there were more than twenty workers, Councils of Trust (*Vertrauensrat*) were set up which were annually elected from lists drawn up by the employers and the shop stewards who were nominated by the Labour Front, but after 1935 no more elections were held because the workers, despite all precautions to the contrary, were electing politically 'unreliable' candidates. A council could theoretically take an employer to the specially created Courts of Social Honour if the local Labour Trustee was convinced that he was maltreating his employees, but this only rarely happened – as is shown by the fact that between 1934 and 1936, out of a labour force of over twenty million, only 616 cases were brought against employers. These courts were thus a poor substitute for trade-union power (**8**(II), **55**).

In his dealings with the workers Hitler had one enormous advantage: he offered them full employment which, according to

Neumann (**60**, p. 431), was his 'sole gift to the masses', and initially there is no doubt that they were grateful for it. Hitler dared not ignore the workers because collectively they represented a powerful source of opposition. Consequently, the Labour Front could not afford to be merely an instrument of oppression. It had both to encourage and to exhort the workers whilst offering them 'an objectified appearance of socialism combining the promises of an emancipation with an extensive depoliticization of industrial relations' (**101**, p. 50). It was essential for it to be seen to be putting into operation what Hitler called 'socialism of the deed'. The Labour Front thus evolved two key departments which owed much to the experiments in welfare capitalism in the 1920s (**55**): the 'Beauty of Work' scheme, run by Albert Speer, aimed with considerable success to modernise and humanise factories by installing modern lighting, swimming baths and canteens; whilst its twin organisation, 'Strength Through Joy', existed mainly to give the workers the opportunity to refresh themselves before making even greater efforts for the *Führer** and Fatherland. The workers were, for example, afforded the chance of cut-price cruises or holidays in ⸢he German countryside. By 1938 a growing number of hotels and even the passenger services of the national railways were becoming economically dependent upon their patronage (**94**).

As the economy, under the stimulus of rearmament, began quickly to absorb the unemployed, Hitler was confronted with a dilemma which was eventually only solved by the widespread use of slave labour in the war (**94**). Hitler needed the support of the workers, but by 1936 the logic of the Four Year Plan was driving him towards controlling both wages and labour. Full employment gave the workers – or at least the skilled workers – a real economic power which they were beginning to exploit, with the consequent danger of spiralling wage costs and crippling labour shortages in the less well-paid industries. Reluctantly and cautiously the regime therefore began to take steps to check the situation. In November 1936 employers were ordered to obtain permission from the labour exchange before taking on more than ten extra men, and workers who left their jobs in breach of contract were threatened with the temporary loss of their work books, which were vital for their further employment. Not surprisingly, the mildness of these measures did little to stop wages leapfrogging in the metal, building and engineering industries, and consequently, in June 1938, the Trustees of Labour were given power to set wage levels in key industries and simultaneously labour conscription was introduced. By August 1939 some 300,000 men had been conscripted to work on the West Wall or on the construction of new factories in central Germany.

Although the growing need to regulate both labour and wages was a consequence of what Mason has called Hitler's failure to overcome 'the stubborn, despairing refusal of the working classes to become the selfless servants of the regime' (**94**, p. 137), the workers' acceptance of the Nazi regime cannot be solely attributed to the undoubted terror of the Gestapo*. Material benefits like longer holidays and low heating and lighting costs did, of course, help buy the workers' acquiescence, but the rise in their standard of living can be exaggerated. The wages of the skilled workers in the metal, engineering and building industries did indeed rise sharply, if overtime and bonus payments are taken into account, but in September 1939 between a quarter and a third of the labour force still drew wages based on the levels current in 1932 (**89**). Although the increasing demand for skilled workers in industry and the chances of a career within the Nazi Party did provide some opportunities for upward mobility for the working classes, Hitler united Germany principally on the basis of what Schoenbaum has so brilliantly described as a 'verbal social revolution' (**102**, p. 52). In Nazi propaganda great emphasis was laid on the nobility of labour and the equality of all Germans. University students were, for example, compelled to do a year's labour service, while Hitler never neglected a chance to show that he valued the workers and peasants at least as highly as the traditional ruling and professional classes. Schoenbaum (**102**) – unlike Laski, Brady (**55**) and Neumann (**60**), who stressed the class character of the Third Reich – argues that Hitler created a genuine though fragile national consensus which was based on the failure of any one class or interest group to dominate.

On balance, it seems that the actual changes in German society do not merit the description 'social revolution'. The Nazi regime in so many areas merely witnessed the continuation of economic and social trends which were common to all advanced societies. Ultimately, of course, by plunging Germany into a war, which it lost, Nazism did pave the way for radical changes after 1945, which arguably really did add up to a social revolution (**164**).

43

9 Nazi Policy towards the Jews, 1933–39

In the debate about the modernity and classlessness of the Nazi state, it is easy, as Burleigh and Wippermann have stressed, to lose sight of the fundamental importance to Hitler of race (**83**). This pervaded every aspect of Nazi policy. Above all, the 'national community' was to be based on a racially homogeneous 'Aryan' people, whose health and racial purity it was vitally important to preserve. The corollary of this new racial unity was the determination by Hitler and his subordinates ultimately not only to eliminate what they regarded as alien racial minorities within Germany, such as the Jews and the Sinti and Roma (gypsies), but also even the mentally ill or incurably handicapped 'Aryan' Germans, of whom over 70,000 were gassed between 1939 and 1941.

Of all the minority groups persecuted by the Nazis, the Jews suffered the worst. Although there were barely 500,000 Jews in Germany in 1933, they were perceived by the Nazis to be the embodiment of evil and the real power behind Bolshevism and thus a major threat to the racial state. Yet, as in so many other areas of government, Nazi policy towards the Jews after the seizure of power was often hesitant and contradictory. The intentionalists, particularly Dawidowicz, Hildebrand and Bracher (**54, 59, 152, 158**), argue that Hitler consistently planned the mass murder of the Jews, even though events might at times have forced him to make tactical retreats. The structuralists, on the other hand, the most prominent of whom are Broszat, Hans Mommsen and Schleunes (**151, 159, 160**), seek rather to find the ultimate cause of the Holocaust in the fragmented and chaotic way in which policy was made in Nazi Germany. Government departments and Nazi leaders, they argue, vied with one another to formulate anti-Semitic policies, and thus set in motion a spiral of ever more radical policies. Understandably, such attempts to depersonalise the responsibility of what ultimately ended in the Holocaust are bitterly resented by the intentionalists, who see such an approach as initiating a new 'cycle of apologetics' (**152**, Intro.) in German history.

After the seizure of power there were no directives issued from

44

the Nazi Party on the Jewish question. Only when independent action by the SA* against individual Jews and their property threatened to escalate uncontrollably and damage his reputation as a responsible statesman did Hitler seek to channel and control the violence by entrusting Streicher, the Gauleiter* of Franconia, with organising a boycott of Jewish shops. The boycott, which occurred on 1 April, was both unpopular in Germany and sharply criticised abroad, particularly in America, and it also risked damaging the German economy as a whole. Hitler therefore sought to deflect the party's anti-Semitism.to less politically and economically sensitive targets. In April 1933 all Jews, with the exception of those who had served or had suffered bereavement in the war, were expelled from the Civil Service and excluded from the universities. Their ejection from journalism was foreshadowed by the setting up of the Reich Chamber of Culture and the Press Law of October 1933 (8(II), **152, 155**).

Intentionalists and structuralists disagree profoundly on Hitler's role in the formulation and execution of these policies (**150**). The structuralists argue that Hitler essentially responded to grass-roots pressure, while the intentionalists emphasise his role as 'stage manager' or 'skilful tactician waiting until the time was ripe before making his next move' (**150**, pp. 4–5). Most historians, however, agree that over the next two years economic and political realities forced Nazi Jewish policy into a relatively moderate mould. For instance, in August 1933 the Foreign and Economic Ministries could only avert a world-wide boycott of German trade planned by international Jewish organisations by negotiating with the Anglo-Palestine bank, which was responsible for the finances of the Zionist movement, an agreement whereby the money of German Jews intending to emigrate to Palestine could be used to purchase imported German goods (**161**). Up to the spring of 1935 the Nazi government discouraged the renewal of overt racial violence and even allowed, for instance, Jewish textile businesses to tender for military contracts.

By the summer of 1935 a mixture of aggressive confidence, fostered by the return of the Saar to the Reich and by the provocative announcement of the German rearmament programme, and of frustration at Hitler's apparent lack of radical drive in domestic policy led to further outbursts of anti-Semitism by party activists. Again the Nazi government responded by seeking to divert anti-Semitic violence into more legal channels. In July 1935 Frick, the Minister of the Interior, circulated a memorandum to the state governments informing them of plans to prohibit marriages between 'Aryans' and 'non-Aryans'. These were announced suddenly and unexpectedly by Hitler at the Nuremberg rally on 13 September. Originally Hitler had intended to speak on foreign policy to the members of the Reichstag*, who had been specially summoned to Nuremberg. When the speech was cancelled on the advice of von Neurath, the Foreign Minister, the notorious Law for the Protection of German Blood forbidding marriage or sexual intercourse between Jews and German gentiles, and the Reich Citizenship Law depriving Jews of their German citizenship, gave Hitler something of substance to announce. Predictably, however, these two laws disappointed many of the hard-liners, who suspected that Hitler had again compromised and accepted the advice of his civil servants rather than of his party activists (**152, 155, 159**).

For the next two years Hitler took no further steps to clarify his anti-Semitic policy. Leading Nazis and government departments competed with one another to fill the vacuum by proposing their own solutions to the Jewish 'problem', each quoting Hitler as their ultimate source of authority. At one inter-ministerial meeting of 17 November 1935, for example, an official from the Ministry of the Interior claimed that Hitler wanted all Jewish emigration halted and the Jews kept as potential hostages in the event of war, while Hess, again quoting Hitler, employed diametrically opposed arguments and insisted that Hitler wished them to emigrate from Germany as quickly as possible (**161**).

By the spring of 1938 the tempo of anti-Semitism was again accelerating. Schacht's resignation from the Economics Ministry in November 1937 ensured that there was now no restraining hand on Göring, when in his role as Commissioner of the Four Year Plan he pressed for the rapid economic expropriation of the Jews. Against the background of the triumphalist mood unleashed by the *Anschluss** of Austria and the growing threat of war with Czechoslovakia, the spring and summer of 1938 witnessed a series of decrees ranging from measures forcing Jews to adopt what the Nazis regarded as specifically Jewish forenames to having their wealth and property registered as a preliminary for expropriation by the state (**152**).

The opportunity to instigate a full-scale pogrom came in November 1938, when Ernst von Rath, a minor diplomat in the German Embassy in Paris, was assassinated by Herschl Grynszpan, a seventeen-year-old student, whose parents had recently been expelled from Germany. Goebbels, apparently with the acquiescence of Hitler, seized the chance to organise what were portrayed to the outside world as spontaneous attacks on synagogues and Jewish-owned businesses. Some 25 million marks' worth of damage was done and nearly 100 Jews were killed, while a further 30,000 were put into concentration camps (**152**). Goebbels' tactics were a direct challenge to both Göring and Himmler, who each had their own plans for solving the Jewish 'problem' (**8(II)**). However, *Krystallnacht* did mark a fresh stage in Nazi policy towards the Jews. With Hitler's support Göring coordinated all initiatives on the Jewish question through his office and began to implement measures for the total expropriation of Jewish property. Not only did the Jews have to pay a collective fee of one and a quarter billion marks, but they were also forced out of the retail trade, skilled labour and management posts. In April 1939 their remaining wealth was confiscated. Decrees, inspired by Goebbels, also barred them from public places, such as theatres and beaches, and the few remaining Jewish children still in state schools were expelled.

In January 1939 the role of the SS* within the various Nazi agencies dealing with the Jews was decisively strengthened. Göring delegated to Heydrich, the Chief of the Security Police and the SD*, responsibility for setting up an organisation modelled on the Central Office for Jewish Emigration, which Eichmann had already established in Vienna, to supervise the emigration of the remaining 214,000 Jews in Germany (see p. 27). Paradoxically, the very success of Göring's expropriation policies made Jewish emigration more difficult to achieve, as no state was willing to accept a large number of impoverished refugees. Heydrich's task was further complicated by the German occupation of Bohemia in March 1939, which increased the number of Jews at the mercy of the Nazis by more than 100,000 (**158**).

Although on 12 November 1938 Hitler apparently instructed Göring both by telephone and through his chief of staff, Bormann, that 'the Jewish question be now once and for all co-ordinated and solved one way or another' (**8(II)**, p. 588), he remained, in public at least, aloof from the numerous anti-Semitic policies initiated in the aftermath of *Krystallnacht*. Nevertheless, on two occasions in January 1939 he was quite specific about the future fate of the Jews. He informed the Czech Foreign Minister of his intention to 'destroy the Jews', and shortly afterwards in the Reichstag* made his notorious prophecy that the outbreak of war would lead to the 'annihilation of the Jewish race in Europe' [**doc. 11(a)**]. To the intentionalists these threats are unambiguous evidence of Hitler's ultimate aims, but the structuralists remain sceptical. They caution historians against interpreting Hitler's words too literally. Mommsen, for instance, stresses that Hitler 'considered the "Jewish question" from a visionary political perspective that did not reflect the real situation' (**159**, p. 112), and argues that Hitler was in fact invoking a ritual hatred of the Jews, rather than expressing definite plans for their murder.

The structuralists are almost certainly correct that Hitler's horrific threats were not precise plans for the Holocaust as it occurred later (**156**), but it is hard not to see them as expressions of intention, however vague and unformulated. As Dawidowicz observed about an earlier speech of Hitler's, 'in the post Auschwitz world' his words carry a 'staggering freight' (**152**, p. 43).

Part Four: Foreign Policy, 1933–45

10 Foreign Policy, 1933–39

No aspect of the history of the Third Reich is more controversial than its foreign policy. Despite the fierce rivalry between the various Nazi agencies over domestic affairs and Hitler's frequent failure to offer a definite lead, there is little doubt that most western historians agree with Rauschning that in foreign affairs it is 'in the last resort Hitler who decides and... does indeed "lead"' (**61**, p. 195). By 1937 at the very latest, neither the Foreign Office nor the armed services were able to exercise any decisive influence on Hitler (**102**), and there is no evidence that either Rosenberg or Ribbentrop ever came permanently near to controlling Nazi foreign policy, although for a time Ribbentrop's views on Britain were listened to by Hitler (**111, 125**). On the other hand, Hitler's policy was not, of course, immune from domestic pressures. Indeed, structuralist historians argue that the development of Nazi foreign policy was primarily influenced by domestic policy. Mommsen, for instance, insists that it was largely an opportunist exercise aimed at enhancing Hitler's image and satisfying the Nazi Party's demand for instant action (**164**). It is certainly true, as Orlow has shown, that in 1938 Hitler's foreign-policy initiatives were particularly welcome to the Nazi Party, which was becoming dangerously impatient of its inability to change German society more rapidly, but then Orlow goes on to stress that there was no 'direct and obvious connection between the radical ferment of the Nazi Party and the foreign-policy initiatives of the German Government' (**73**(II), p. 230). Similar objections can be applied to Mason's argument that by the end of 1937 the German economy was facing grave financial and labour problems which could only be solved in the context of a victorious war. Despite Mason's impressive articles on the subject (**94, 124**), the historian is hard put to pin-point 'any causal relation between Hitler's awareness of the deepening crisis and the gathering pace of German foreign policy after 1937' (**110**, p. 65).

   Inevitably much of the debate on German foreign policy during the Third Reich is concentrated on the aims and motives of Adolf

Hitler. Rauschning's thesis that Hitler's ultimate aim was simply the 'maximum of power and dominion' (**61**, p. 284) was power- fully endorsed by Alan Bullock in the first edition (1952) of his biography of Hitler when he observed that 'Hitler had only one programme, power without limit, and the rest was window dressing' (**38**, p. 448).[1] This view of Hitler as a manic expansionist was rejected by Trevor-Roper, who argued that *Mein Kampf* was 'a complete blueprint of his intended achievements and in no significant point different from its ultimate actual form' (**4**, Intro.). He stressed that Hitler was a systematic thinker whose ideas must therefore be taken as seriously as Bismarck's or Lenin's, and drew the conclusion from *Mein Kampf* (**1**) and *Hitler's Table Talk* (**4**) that the conquest of *Lebensraum** in Russia was the overriding aim of Hitler's foreign policy [**doc. 12a**]. Thus up to 1960 the great majority of historians did not doubt that Hitler intended war. The only debate was whether his aims were global or continental. However, in 1961 Taylor, in his brilliant and seminal study on the origins of the Second World War, attempted to demythologise Hitler by arguing that 'his foreign policy was that of his predecessors, of the professional diplomats at the Foreign Ministry and virtually all Germans' and was aimed at making Germany 'the greatest power in Europe from her natural weight' (**131**, p. 68). He categorically dismissed the possibility that Hitler was a system-maker 'deliberately preparing...a great war which would destroy existing civilization and make him master of the world', and insisted that Hitler was a pragmatist whose foreign policy was to a great extent a reaction to the initiatives of other powers.

Taylor's views unleashed a passionate debate which still rever- berates. His most radical critics have been among the German historians of the 'Programme school' led by Andreas Hillgruber (**116**) and Klaus Hildebrand (**115**), who argue that Hitler's foreign policy was formulated in the mid-1920s and remained 'remarkably consistent...in spite of his flexible approach to details' (**117**, p. 7). They claim that Hitler's programme consisted of two main phases: the continental phase, which would involve the defeat of France and the conquest of European Russia, and then the global phase, which would establish Germany as a world power through the annexation of colonial territories, the construction of a large

---

[1]Subsequently he revised his sentence to read: 'Hitler had only one programme: power, first his own power in Germany, and then the expan- sion of German power in Europe' (**38**, 1962 edn, ch. 8, p. 489).

navy and the defeat of the United States. In the first phase Britain and Italy were to be allotted the key role of allies, whereas in the second phase Hitler realised that he might well have to face British hostility, although he apparently hankered after a global partnership with the British Empire. The Programme thesis depends primarily on a close reading of *Mein Kampf* (1) and *Hitler's Secret Book* (2). In both books Hitler outlined his plans for the conquest of *Lebensraum** [doc. 12a] in Russia after the defeat of France, which he hoped to achieve with the assistance of a British and Italian alliance [doc. 12b]. But Hillgruber, by emphasising Hitler's tacit assumption that the new Germanic super-race would inherit the earth and his criticism of Wilhelmine foreign policy [doc. 12c], argues, not always convincingly, that 'contrary to the opinion of many historians, the essentials of the idea of overseas expansion were already covertly indicated in *Mein Kampf* (117, p. 10).

Taylor and the proponents of the Programme thesis have adopted diametrically opposed interpretations, both of which in their turn have been subjected to considerable criticism. Although Taylor has forced historians to rethink the causes of the Second World War, with the result that many have modified their original views, he is nevertheless open to the criticism that he has underestimated the revolutionary content of Nazi ideas. Taylor blandly ignores the fact that the Nazi government 'systematically militarized all social relations, turned employers and workers into "leaders and followers", had its youth do rifle drill with spades, elevated fanaticism into the supreme public virtue and saw all facets of life as struggles or battles for existence and domination' (124, p. 109). The precise arguments of the Programme school also lose some of their credibility when it is remembered that in domestic affairs the Nazis so often carried out the opposite of what they preached. Hans Mommsen is therefore fully justified in questioning 'whether National Socialist foreign policy can be considered an unchanging pursuit of established priorities' (71, p. 177).

The bewildering contradiction between Hitler's long-term objectives and short-term pragmatism was to a certain extent reconciled by Alan Bullock in 1967 when he argued that Nazi foreign policy was only comprehensible if it was seen as combining 'consistency of aim with complete opportunism in method and tactics' (109, p. 193). Whilst most historians agree that Hitler was aiming, at the very least, to reclaim the territory Germany won from Russia at the Treaty of Brest-Litovsk in 1918 but lost again at

Versailles, there is less agreement about the nature of his global policy. It is, however, arguable that economic needs alone would have pushed Hitler into such a policy. Hitler's grandiose building and reconstruction plans for the Third Reich, for example, could only have been implemented once he commanded the economic resources of a world-wide empire (**132**). Given Hitler's reluctance to tolerate limits to his power, it is most unlikely that his foreign policy would have remained purely continental once Russia was defeated.

Hitler's immediate priorities in 1933, apart from safeguarding the new Nazi regime from foreign intervention, were to destroy the Versailles settlement, rearm, dismantle the French alliance system in eastern Europe, and escape from isolation by securing alliances with Britain and Italy. Only then would he be able successfully to confront France and gain a free hand against Russia. In 1933 Germany was both economically and militarily weak, but the realities of world politics in fact favoured a revival of German power: the world slump confirmed American isolation, France had never properly recovered its nerve after failing to coerce Germany in the Ruhr in 1923, and Britain, menaced by Japan in the Far East and weakened by the incipient break-up of its empire, was deeply reluctant to defend the *status quo* of 1919. Hitler also had the luck to come to power at a time when the serious revision of the Versailles settlement had already begun. In 1929–30 Britain and France evacuated the Rhineland, and in 1932 German reparation payments were effectively cancelled at the Lausanne Conference.

Preferring the freedom of action that only bilateral pacts could afford him, Hitler was anxious to avoid becoming enmeshed in multilateral disarmament agreements or regional pacts. In October 1933, with minimal risks, he was able to exploit Anglo-French differences and walk out of both the Disarmament Conference and the League of Nations. To avoid provoking retaliation he had consistently stressed his desire for peace, and in June he had even signed a four-power pact proposed by Mussolini aimed at achieving a peaceful revision of Versailles, gambling correctly on the hunch that French opposition would ultimately prevent its ratification. In January 1934 Hitler achieved a considerable diplomatic success with the signing of the non-aggression pact with Poland. There is little doubt that it was a major breach in the French alliance system in eastern Europe and freed Hitler from immediate pressure on his eastern frontiers, although paradoxically it accelerated a Franco-Russian *rapprochement* (**110**). It is possible, as the Programme school asserts, that Hitler envisaged an eventual Polish alliance either against France or Russia (**115**), but it seems more likely that 'ultimately there was no place for an independent Poland in Hitler's Europe: the most she could hope for was the position of a vassal state' (**38**, p. 325).

Hitler was less successful in his pursuit of British and Italian alliances. Mussolini was suspicious of Hitler's designs on Austria, and consequently German–Italian relations deteriorated sharply when the Austrian Nazis, with tacit backing from Berlin, staged an unsuccessful coup in Vienna in July 1934 and Mussolini retaliated by moving troops up to the Austrian frontier (**114, 138**). As early as April 1933 Hitler had indirectly begun to approach the British about an alliance, but no progress was made until February 1935 when Britain, responding to reports on the growth of the *Luftwaffe**, began to sound out Germany about joining an Anglo-French air pact, which would set mutually agreed limits to the size of national air forces. British reaction to German rearmament was an attempt to moderate it by agreement rather than by coercion. Hitler had thus little to fear when he announced the reintroduction of conscription, even though France, Italy and Britain met at Stresa and condemned the German action. Hitler quickly countered by assuring the powers of his peaceful intentions and then offered to conclude bilateral disarmament pacts with his neighbours. The British government seized on the chance to negotiate a naval convention which limited the German navy to 35 per cent of the strength of the Royal Navy. Their unilateral action broke up the unity of the Stresa front and, by implying British approval of German rearmament, 'set in motion the momentous chain of events that prevented a possible anti-Hitler coalition and freed the Third Reich from the threat of isolation' (**54**, p. 369). British and German interpretations of the convention differed markedly: to Hitler it was a first step towards an alliance, whereas the British cabinet saw it primarily as a means of taming Hitler and ultimately drawing him back into the League of Nations (**115**).

Although German–Italian relations were already improving, it was Mussolini's attack on Ethiopia in October 1935 and his subsequent break with the Entente powers which had imposed sanctions on Italy, that accelerated cooperation between Rome and Berlin and also provided Hitler with the chance to take the vital step of remilitarising the Rhineland. Until January 1936 Hitler maintained a neutral position and even sold arms to the

Ethiopians. However, to avoid complete isolation, Mussolini was driven to approach Hitler and to secure his goodwill by intimating that Italy would not prevent Austria from becoming, in due course, a German satellite. Hitler was therefore able to extract further assurances from Mussolini in February that he would not oppose the remilitarisation of the Rhineland. Despite the ratification of the Franco-Soviet treaty on 27 February 1936 by the French parliament, Hitler gambled correctly on Anglo-French inaction and reoccupied the Rhineland with a weak military force which would almost certainly have been withdrawn had allied troops intervened. The remilitarisation of the Rhineland has been described as 'a real turning point in the inter-war years which marked the beginning of a shift in the balance of power away from Paris and back to Berlin' (**111**, pp. 126–7). It deprived France of its main strategic advantage over Germany and showed that neither Britain nor France had the will to defend the Versailles Treaty.

Despite the virtual collapse of the Versailles system by 1936, Germany's military weakness prevented Hitler from making any more major advances in the immediate future. Nevertheless, in August 1936 he refused to let the acute balance of payments crisis slow down the tempo of rearmament and personally intervened to set up the Four Year Plan with the expressed intention of preparing both the army and the economy for war against Bolshevism within four years. It is quite possible that the tone of Hitler's memorandum was influenced by the need to overcome opposition to rearmament within Germany, but it is also surely a clear expression of his ultimate intentions and of his ideological hatred of Bolshevism (**110**) [**doc. 6**].

The outbreak of the Spanish Civil War in July 1936 strengthened Germany's position considerably. The war, which rapidly became seen as an ideological conflict between Left and Right, divided Europe and exacerbated mutual suspicions between Britain and France on the one hand and Soviet Russia on the other, and so hindered the building of a firm anti-Nazi front. As both Hitler and Mussolini gave support to Franco the war cemented German–Italian cooperation, which was given more precise form in the October Protocols (1936). In November Hitler signed the Anti-Comintern Pact with Japan, which was a vague agreement aimed against the Communist International rather than Soviet Russia. Although Hitler gained important economic concessions from Franco, his purposes were best solved by the continuation of the conflict, as it distracted the west from central Europe and also gave him a chance to play on British fears of growing Bolshevik influence in Spain (**114**). In October 1936 Ribbentrop was sent to London specifically to secure a British alliance. He failed, but continuing British passivity in the face of German and Italian involvement in Spain led Hitler to believe that Britain might well tolerate German expansion in eastern Europe (**110**). By the end of 1937 Germany's diplomatic position had improved. When Italy joined the Anti-Comintern Pact in November, a new power bloc seemed to be in the making, which could threaten Britain and France simultaneously in the Far East and in Europe. German rearmament was also progressing quickly, while the divisions and distractions among its potential enemies had greatly increased. Taylor has argued that Hitler, after his success in dismantling the Versailles and Locarno systems, 'was at a loss what to do next even after he had the power to do it' (**131**, p. 108). It was claimed by the Allies at the Nuremberg trials and by the immediate post-war generation of historians that Hitler produced a complete blueprint of aims at a secret meeting at the Reich Chancellery on 5 November, the minutes of which were recorded by Colonel Hossbach (**126**(1)) [**doc. 13**]. Hitler stressed that his overriding aim was to acquire *Lebensraum** within Europe rather than the colonies, at the latest by the period 1943–45, but indicated that he would move against Czechoslovakia and Austria before this date if France were distracted either by a civil war or hostilities with Italy. Taylor claims forcefully that Hitler's notorious exposition was for the most part 'day dreaming, unrelated to what followed in real life', and that the meeting was called primarily for domestic purposes (**131**, p. 132). Today, the majority of historians concede that the meeting resulted from Hitler having to arbitrate between the rival claims of Blomberg and Göring over the allocation of raw materials and that he may well have exaggerated the possibility of war in order to goad the generals on to accepting a faster tempo of rearmament (**110**), but 'the consensus still favours the view that Hitler was serving notice on Blomberg and Fritsch that a more adventurous and dangerous phase in foreign policy was imminent' (**111**, p. 128).

Surprisingly, Hitler did not mention his most important aim – the colonisation of western Russia. Noakes and Pridham argue that this omission was deliberate 'in order not to frighten his audience with the prospects of war on two fronts' (**8**,[1] p. 521), but Koch sees

---

[1]1974 single volume edition.

it as crucial evidence to support his argument that between 1933 and 1939 Hitler was more concerned with restoring Germany's pre-1914 frontiers than with expanding into Russia (**119**). Hildebrand, on the other hand, accepts without argument Hitler's deadline of 1943–45 as 'the relatively accurate timing for the carrying out of the continental stage within the *Stufenplan**' (**115**, p. 52). To the Programme school, however, the real significance of the Hossbach memorandum lies in the fact that Britain was now bracketed with France as a 'hate-inspired antagonist' and that Hitler was clearly contemplating pursuing his eastern European ambitions without a British alliance, although he still hoped for neutrality. Norman Rich (**126**(1)) is convinced that Hitler had already decided to knock out both France and Britain before attacking Russia and was thus contemplating eliminating Austria and Czechoslovakia before turning westwards. Historians' interpretations of Hitler's remarks thus vary widely, but most would agree with Mason that 'the conference marks the point at which the expansion of the Third Reich ceased to be latent and became explicit' (**124**, p. 114). It is significant, for example, that a month later General Jodl, the Chief of the Operations Staff, drew up plans for an offensive rather than defensive war against Czechoslovakia.

The opportunities to annex Austria and to dismember Czechoslovakia were presented to Hitler both more quickly than he envisaged and in a diplomatic situation that differed markedly from the scenario he had outlined on 5 November. The *Anschluss** was a 'striking example' of Hitler's ability to combine 'consistency in aim, calculation and patience in preparation with opportunism, impulse and improvisation in execution' (**109**, p. 204). By January 1938 Hitler had made considerable progress in the gradual absorption of Austria. Despite the failure of 1934 the Austrian Nazis had done much to undermine the state from within and Mussolini had come round to conceding Hitler a free hand in Austria, while the new Chamberlain government was openly talking about 'alterations in the European status quo' in Danzig, Austria and Czechoslovakia (**131**). However, the actual timing of the *Anschluss* was not Hitler's. When Schuschnigg, the Austrian Chancellor, on his own initiative sought out Hitler in an attempt to curb Nazi agitation within Austria, Hitler seized the chance to dictate a series of conditions which effectively turned Austria into a German satellite. It was only Schuschnigg's desperate attempt on 9 March to regain a measure of independence from Hitler by asking his countrymen to vote in a referendum for a 'free and German, independent and social, Christian and united Austria' that prompted Hitler to drop his policy of gradual absorption and on 12 March to invade with an army that was so ill-prepared that it left 'along its path a trail of stranded vehicles' (**133**, p. 46). Faced with a tumultuous reception at Linz, Hitler quickly abandoned his original idea of installing a satellite government under Seyss-Inquart and instead incorporated Austria into the Reich.

After the annexation of Austria without any international repercussions, Czechoslovakia, which Hitler regarded alternately as a French or Russian aircraft carrier in the middle of Europe, became more vulnerable to German pressure. While it possessed a well-equipped army and efficient armaments industry, its potential strength was undermined by its ethnically divided population. Its unity was above all menaced by the three million Sudeten Germans who increasingly wished to be included in the Third Reich.

Until late May 1938 Hitler had no immediate plan for attacking Czechoslovakia. He may have been waiting for the kind of international distraction in the west which he had forecast at the meeting on 5 November 1937 or for the conclusion of a definite military pact with Italy before committing himself (**134**). On 28 March 1938 Henlein, the Sudeten German leader, was instructed by Hitler to formulate demands for Sudeten home rule which would appear reasonable to outside observers, but which the Czechs could not accept without risking the break-up of their state. On the weekend of 20–21 May the Czech government completely surprised Hitler by partially mobilising its army in response to inaccurate rumours of an imminent German attack which, significantly, Britain, France and Russia made clear they would not tolerate. Hitler proclaimed his innocence, but paradoxically this false alarm, far from deterring him, persuaded him to set 1 October as the deadline for 'smashing Czechoslovakia'. Taylor dismisses this as mere bluff, arguing that 'Hitler did not need to act. Others would do his work for him' (**131**, p. 152). It is of course correct that in response to Hitler's threats Chamberlain did come forward, but surely Bullock again shows a more realistic interpretation when he stresses that Hitler kept his options open 'to the very last possible moment' (**109**, p. 208). Throughout the summer of 1938 Hitler continued to encourage Sudeten separatism, and in early September he finalised his military plans for localised action against Czechoslovakia. On 12 September he bitterly attacked Czechoslovakia in a virulent speech at Nuremberg which provoked a Sudeten uprising and the subsequent intervention of Chamberlain, who believed war to be imminent. At Berchtesgaden Hitler, by both stressing his desire for Anglo-German cooperation and threatening war, strengthened Chamberlain's readiness to agree to the peaceful cession of the Sudetenland to Germany. When Chamberlain again met Hitler at Bad Godesberg on 22 September, after gaining French approval for his initiative, he was confronted with the unacceptable demand for the almost immediate German occupation of the Sudetenland, which Hitler only on the following day reluctantly postponed to 1 October. It is impossible to determine precisely why Hitler suddenly presented what was in effect an ultimatum. While Taylor argues that he was procrastinating in order to give the Hungarians and Poles the chance to formulate their own territorial demands on Czechoslovakia, thereby giving himself an admirable pretext for intervening as 'a peace-maker to create a new order' (**131**, p. 179), it is possible that he was seriously considering war. Arguably (**22**), the more Hitler increased his demands, the greater was the chance that the Czechs would reject them and be abandoned by the British and French to the military solution which Hitler basically favoured. But in the face of partial British and French mobilisation and the obvious desire of his generals and Mussolini to avoid war, Hitler finally consented to the Munich conference, as a consequence of which Germany was at last permitted to occupy the Sudetenland in stages between 1 and 10 October 1938.

Although Churchill's damning criticism of Munich is hard to fault, Chamberlain had at least succeeded in stopping unilateral German action and in securing a four-power guarantee for rump-Czechoslovakia. Thus Hitler apparently interpreted the conference as a diplomatic defeat which cheated him of Czechoslovakia and as a sign that Britain, despite its willingness to appease, would not allow Germany a completely free hand in eastern Europe (**110, 115**). It is therefore significant that on 21 October 1938 the German army was told to draw up plans for the final defeat of Czechoslovakia. Hitler used the separatist demands of the Slovaks as his Trojan horse to provoke the break-up of the Czech state. While it is true that the actual timing of the crisis in March 1939 may again have taken Hitler by surprise, he speedily exploited the situation which he had done so much to provoke by forcing President Hacha to agree to the German occupation of Prague and the creation of an independent Slovakia which was in fact a German protectorate.

In early 1939 it could be said that Hitler 'had lost his bearings' (**111**, p. 132) and momentarily did not know where next to turn. In December 1938 he had started to cultivate good relations with France by recognising its western frontiers, and in January he unsuccessfully sounded out the Polish government on the return of Danzig and a German road and rail link through the Corridor in return for eventual Polish gains in the Ukraine. While he was primarily contemplating an attack on Russia, Polish support would also have freed him to turn westwards should he decide to knock out France and Britain first (**8**(III)). In January he also gave orders for the construction of a large navy, which was to be ready by the mid-1940s and he had plans drawn up for the seizure of colonial territory in Africa. It would thus seem that he was already contemplating the war against the British Empire and perhaps America which, according to the Programme school, would occur after the defeat of Russia (**115**).

However, the Anglo-French guarantee of Poland on 30 March 1939, which was a consequence of the dismemberment of Czechoslovakia, made Hitler decide to concentrate on the Polish problem. Arguably, the guarantee, which was undoubtedly 'a revolutionary event in international affairs' (**131**, p. 215), convinced Hitler that war was now unavoidable if he was to continue with his expansionary policy. There is certainly ample evidence that Hitler ordered his generals to draw up detailed plans for operations against Poland to be carried out any time after 1 September. On 23 May 1939, for example, he categorically stated that he wished 'to attack Poland at the first suitable opportunity'. (**8** (III), p. 738) Taylor (**131**) and Koch may of course be correct that he was only talking 'for effect' (**119**, p. 174) in the hope that he would persuade Britain and France to abandon Poland, but it has been shown (**110**) that Hitler's generals and ministers were convinced that war was imminent.

The second 'revolutionary event' of the summer of 1939 was the Nazi-Soviet Non-Aggression Treaty of 23 August, which, by securing Russia's benevolent neutrality in return for territorial concessions in eastern Europe, deprived Britain and France of the only alliance which could have stopped Poland's defeat. Hitler was now understandably confident that he had minimised the danger of western intervention and planned to attack Poland on 26 August. When, however, Britain and France stubbornly ratified their treaties of guarantee instead of abandoning Poland, Hitler postponed the attack and made several attempts to persuade

Britain to repeat its Munich policy. On 29 August Hitler insisted that the British should arrange for the Poles to send to Berlin a minister with full powers to negotiate a settlement by the following day. Although the British desired negotiations, they refused to press the Poles to obey what was in reality an ultimatum, and consequently, on 31 August, at 12.30, Hitler gave the order for war. Taylor insists that the war began because Hitler launched 'on 29 August a diplomatic manoeuvre which he ought to have launched on 28 August' (**131**, p. 278). It is perhaps possible that, given more time, he might have driven a wedge between Britain and Poland, but it is more likely that, faced with the approaching prospect of the autumn rains, which threatened the success of a *Blitzkrieg**, he lost patience and decided to unleash a war which he had long contemplated.

11 Foreign Policy, 1939–45

Between September 1939 and December 1941 Hitler kept both the diplomatic and military initiative and followed a policy which in the short term at any rate was realistic and pragmatic. However, once his *Blitzkrieg** tactics failed, his flexibility deserted him and he pursued a blindly destructive and purely ideological course which ended in the total defeat of the Third Reich.

Although Hitler had taken the risk of a two-front war in September 1939, Anglo-French military passivity enabled him to destroy an isolated Poland in six weeks. His triumph was greatly facilitated by the Nazi-Soviet Pact, which however also strengthened Russia's western frontiers by recognising Finland, the Baltic states, eastern Poland and Romanian Bessarabia as belonging to the Russian sphere of interest, thereby creating an effective barrier, that was only breached in northern Bukovina, between Hitler and the Ukraine. Most historians agree that Hitler had no immediate territorial aims in western Europe and that he wished merely to eliminate western opposition before attacking Russia. The key to future success in the east was to gain the acquiescence of Britain. Hildebrand persuasively argues that Hitler 'regarded the war against Britain as yet another attempt, this time using military means, to draw into the German camp a Britain who had stubbornly refused to give in' (**115**, p. 94). Hitler could either attempt to come to terms with Britain and France or defeat them. Initially at any rate, Hitler kept both options open. On 6 October he proposed a negotiated peace on the basis of a new order in Poland, which was rejected, and simultaneously prepared for an attack in the west. Hitler did not contemplate a long war against Britain and did little to build up a submarine fleet. In April 1940 he belatedly occupied Norway, which gave the German navy important bases for operations in the North Atlantic, only because Britain itself was about to land troops there and threaten German iron ore supplies.

Throughout the winter of 1939–40 Germany received considerable economic and even military assistance from Soviet Russia

(136). Russia's supplies of vital raw materials, the use of its railway system to transport rubber from the Far East and the protection given to German merchantmen all helped neutralise the economic consequences of the British blockade. In exchange for supplies of German naval equipment Stalin also offered the Germans a naval base near Murmansk. At this stage of the war Hitler appreciated Soviet assistance, and when Russia attacked Finland, he had, contrary to his most deeply held beliefs, to exert considerable pressure on Mussolini to stop him supplying the Finns with aircraft. Ironically, it was probably only Russian assistance that prevented an early German economic collapse and enabled Hitler to mount the devastating *Blitzkrieg** in May 1940, which drove Britain from the Continent and forced France to request an armistice on 16 June.

In June and July 1940 Hitler attempted to pave the way for a British peace initiative (126(1)). As early as 13 June he assured the British that it had never been his intention to destroy their empire, and on 19 July he stressed in the Reichstag* that there was now no reason for the continuation of the war. When his offer was again rejected on 22 July he became increasingly perplexed and vacillated half-heartedly between a number of courses, all designed to force Britain into making peace. On 16 July Hitler issued his first detailed directive preparing for the invasion of Britain, but the Germans failed to achieve the essential preconditions for such an operation, the preliminary destruction of British sea and air power. Despite these preparations few would disagree with Hildebrand's assertion that Hitler 'was never absolutely and genuinely prepared to agree wholeheartedly to an invasion' (115, p. 103). Quite apart from his 'doctrinaire inclination towards his British enemy' (115, p. 103), he was wary of undertaking a hazardous military operation while Russia was still undefeated in the east [doc. 14].

Hitler was urged by both his army and navy to attack Britain's lines of communication through the Mediterranean by supporting Italian operations in North Africa and by aiding anti-British movements in the Arab world with the support of Vichy France. Hitler certainly explored these possibilities, but despite the very real diplomatic difficulties he encountered it is hard not to agree with Field-Marshal Kesselring that Hitler 'disastrously undervalued the Mediterranean's importance' (112, p. 87). In the autumn of 1940, in 'what may have been the most important diplomatic discussions of the war' (126(2), p. 217), Hitler made serious attempts to persuade Franco and Marshal Pétain, the Minister-President of Vichy France, to enter the war against Britain. At a meeting with Franco at Hendaye on 23 October 1940 he tried to secure Spain's cooperation in seizing Gibraltar, but Franco refused to abandon neutrality unless he was guaranteed a large part of French North Africa, a request which Hitler could hardly grant if he wished to win over Vichy France. On 24 October Hitler met Pétain at Montoire but, despite assurances that he accepted the principle of collaboration with Germany, Pétain skilfully avoided any actual military commitment. It is possible that Hitler might have won him over if he had negotiated a generous peace treaty, but Hitler was unwilling to make a final settlement with France until the defeat of Britain and was also handicapped by having privately assured Mussolini that Nice, Corsica, Tunis and French Somaliland would in due course fall to Italy (**126**(2)). Hitler cynically but correctly observed that 'the resolution of the conflicting interests of France, Italy and Spain in Africa is only possible through a grandiose fraud' (**112**, p. 89).

Hitler's difficulties in the Mediterranean were increased by Mussolini's incompetent attempts to emulate Germany's military achievements. Although Mussolini had declared war on Britain and France on 10 June 1940, German and Italian strategy was never effectively coordinated. Mussolini's expressed aim was to fight 'not for Germany but only for Italy alongside Germany' (**8**(III), p. 793), and consequently he was initially reluctant to accept German offers of help to occupy Egypt. It was only when the Italians were threatened with a complete rout by the British in December and January 1940–41 that German troops under Rommel were sent. Rommel's achievements in the next eighteen months were impressive and show what a larger German force could have brought about if it had been dispatched earlier.

Prodded on by Ribbentrop, Hitler also explored the chance of creating an anti-British Continental power bloc (**115**). On 27 September a Tripartite Pact was signed between Italy, Japan and Germany, in which the three powers not only recognised their respective spheres of interest in Europe and eastern Asia but, in a clause that was aimed at the United States, also undertook 'to assist one another with all political, economic and military means' should one of them be attacked by a power not currently involved in hostilities in Europe or China. Hungary, Romania and Slovakia all joined the pact, but in November 1940 Ribbentrop failed to persuade Molotov to accept what Cecil has called 'a junior partnership in an international crime syndicate' (**112**, p. 107). Molotov, the Soviet Foreign Minister, stressed with an embarrassing clarity that Russia was not prepared to forget its traditional interests in Turkey, south-eastern and central Europe. The Tripartite Pact soon proved to have little real value. It failed to deter the United States from stepping up its naval and economic cooperation with Britain or to dissuade Japan from seriously considering a *rapprochement* with the United Sates in early 1941.

While Hitler was preparing for an invasion of Britain and toying with alternatives in the Mediterranean, he had already instructed his generals to prepare plans for an attack on Russia. By early August 1940 a growing number of troops were being transferred eastwards, and on 18 December he finally decided to launch the Russian invasion in the spring of 1941. His reasons for taking this fatal step at the time he did are by no means clear. Of course, the destruction of Bolshevik Russia was one of his major aims, but by leaving an undefeated Britain increasingly backed by a powerful United States in the west he committed the very strategic error he had sworn to avoid in *Mein Kampf.* Weinberg argues that the 'decision to attack the Soviet Union was Hitler's answer to the challenge of England – as it had been Napoleon's' (**136**, p. 171). At a conference on 31 July 1940 [**doc. 14**] Hitler sought to convince his generals that the defeat of the Soviet Union would at a stroke deprive Britain of the hope of both a Russian and an American alliance and consequently bring about its capitulation. Although there were certainly formidable obstacles in the way of defeating Britain, it is nevertheless true that Hitler was 'pursuing an indirect approach of a singular kind' (**112**, p. 78). If the defeat of Britain had really been his first priority, he would surely have concentrated on intensifying the naval war and on attacking Britain in the Mediterranean with adequate forces. Perhaps it is therefore more accurate to say that the defeat of Britain was only a 'subsidiary aim of the Russian offensive' (**117**, p. 17).

Rich argues that Hitler attacked the Soviet Union because he believed that Stalin would 'never tolerate a definitive German victory in the west' (**126**(1), p. 204). It is true that Stalin by 1941 was in a position, both economically and militarily, to threaten Germany. He had exploited the Nazi-Soviet Pact to build up the Russian position in eastern Europe, and by annexing northern Bukovina and Bessarabia in June 1940 was poised to strike at the Romanian oilfields on which the Nazi war machine depended.

Hitler had been sufficiently worried to send troops into the oilfields in September 1940, which in turn prompted Stalin to raise the question of Russian interests in Finland and Bulgaria. Rich also stressed that as the Soviet Union either directly supplied the Nazis with most of their raw materials or allowed them to be transported across its territory, Stalin could at any time strangle Germany economically. However, this argument can be countered by pointing out that the USSR profited from its trade with Germany and had every incentive to keep the peace (**112**). In June 1941 there was no evidence that Stalin was planning a war against Germany in the near future. Hitler's decision to attack Russia cannot be properly understood unless it is seen in the context of Nazi ideology. His belief in his mission to destroy Bolshevism and to provide *Lebensraum** (**docs 6, 12a, 13**) is the real motive force behind the invasion. He had planned the operation carefully, and as Bullock emphasises, 'of all decisions it is the one which most clearly bears his own personal stamp, the culmination (as he saw it) of his career' (**109**, p. 218).

Before Hitler could launch the attack he had to secure his south-eastern flank. Mussolini, contrary to Hitler's desire to keep the Balkans quiet, had attacked but failed to defeat Greece in the winter of 1940–41, and consequently gave the British an opportunity to land and establish air bases which could seriously threaten the southern flank of a German offensive in Russia (**126**(1), **138**). In December Hitler had decided in principle to assist Mussolini, and by March he had secured Balkan support for German intervention, when the pro-German regime in Yugoslavia was overthrown in favour of a more anglophile administration. Hitler responded by a *Blitzkrieg** which ended on 23 April with the defeat of both Greece and Yugoslavia and secured the whole of south-east Europe as a base for military operations against Russia, which were launched on 22 June.

Hitler was so convinced that Russia could be defeated in a matter of weeks that he had not bothered to attempt to coordinate a Japanese attack on Siberia, an elementary omission which Ribbentrop tried in vain to rectify once the invasion had started (**115**). When the *Blitzkrieg** was finally halted by the Russians before Moscow in December 1941, Hitler was faced with the prospect of a long-drawn-out war on two fronts. Then simultaneously the European war escalated into a world war when Japan attacked the American fleet at Pearl Harbor. As Japan was the aggressor Germany was not theoretically committed to assist it by the Tripartite Pact (**8**(III)), but Hitler seized the chance to declare war on the United States and to give Japan every encouragement to tie the Americans down in the Pacific. He gambled on the Pacific war preventing the United States from helping Britain in the west and on leaving him free to defeat Russia (**115**). In the light of Anglo-American cooperation in 1940–41 he saw a declaration of war as merely formalising what in fact existed already.

In the summer of 1942 German troops in the Soviet Union advanced as far as the Caucasus, and for a few months it seemed as if the German-Japanese agreement of 18 January 1942 to divide up the eastern hemisphere would be realised. After defeating the USSR, Hitler intended to turn on the United States with Japanese help, although there is no doubt that he still hankered after a British alliance which he believed a Soviet defeat and Japanese pressure on India might bring about (**115, 117**).

However, in the autumn and winter of 1942–43 Hitler finally lost the initiative at Stalingrad and El Alamein and was remorselessly pushed on the defensive in both the east and the west. In July 1943 British and American troops landed in Sicily and Mussolini was deposed in Rome, while the German offensive at Kursk on the eastern front was decisively broken. Almost a year later the Allies landed in Normandy and by January 1945 the Soviet army was only 60 kilometres east of Berlin. Hitler responded to these blows by fighting defensively in the west and by irrationally hoping for a decisive victory in the east which would cause Britain to negotiate a settlement. He rejected the peace feelers put forward by Stalin in 1942 and 1943, although in 1944 he did show a certain interest in attempts by the Japanese to mediate on his behalf with the Russians (**115, 120**). Basically, however, he preferred peace with the west, and at the end of the war he was desperately hoping that a split would develop between the Russians and the Americans. But he was battering against a closed door, because the western Allies had already agreed at Casablanca in January 1943 to hold out for the unconditional surrender of the Axis powers. Nazi atrocities strengthened the resolve of the west to defeat Germany, while Hitler's ideological crusade in the east blinded him to the chances of yet another deal with Stalin.

12 German-occupied Europe, 1939–45

In 1942, except for a few islands of neutrality, Hitler's continental empire stretched from the Pyrenees to the Caucasus and from Norway to the Mediterranean. Hitler was, however, too preoccupied with winning the war to produce a uniform plan for administering Europe and instead adopted a series of *ad hoc* solutions more or less tailored to local circumstances (**126**(2), **139**).

In the west he annexed little territory outright, although in the long term he undoubtedly harboured more ambitious plans. From Belgium he took Eupen and Malmédy, which had been German up to 1918, and he absorbed Luxembourg, Alsace and most of Lorraine administratively into the Reich. Hitler regarded the Scandinavians and the Dutch as Germanic peoples who would in due course find a permanent place in the Greater German Reich. When German troops occupied Norway, Denmark and Holland in 1940, Hitler had originally hoped to cooperate with the existing governments and work through them to secure essential German interests, but only in Denmark did this policy meet with initial success. Both the Norwegian and Dutch monarchs fled to London with their cabinets, and Hitler had to install *Reichskommissaren** – who were, however, able to rule through the existing administrative machinery and only needed a relatively small number of German bureaucrats to assist them. For a time Denmark was the showpiece of Nazi Europe. King, cabinet and parliament appeared to function normally and in March 1943 there was even a general election, but this was in fact only a façade for indirect German rule. Danish economic and foreign policy were both dictated from Berlin, and when the elections produced a large majority against collaboration with Hitler the German authorities seized the opportunity provided by strikes and sabotage to declare martial law.

Belgium was also deemed to be a Germanic country which would eventually be dissolved into two new *Reichsgaue*, Flanders and Brabant, but up to July 1944 it was administered, together with the two French departments of Nord and Pas de Calais, by a military government as it was an essential base for military

Europe at the height of Nazi power, 1942

operations against Britain. Hitler devised 'a remarkably clever arrangement' (**126**(2), p. 200) to protect German interests in France, by dividing France into the occupied and unoccupied zones. The French government, which remained at Vichy in the unoccupied zone, saved German manpower by administering the whole country, but could at any time be put under pressure by the mere threat of tightening up on border restrictions between the two zones.

In south-eastern Europe Hitler had few territorial ambitions. Romania, Bulgaria and Hungary were German satellites. After the defeat of Yugoslavia and Greece, Hitler annexed the former Austrian territories in Slovenia, but broke up Yugoslavia into three small countries, Croatia, Serbia and Montenegro, where puppet regimes were installed as façades for German and Italian rule. A weak collaborationist government was tolerated in Greece, which Hitler regarded as primarily within the Italian sphere of interest. Only in 1943, after Mussolini's fall, did German troops take over full responsibility for the occupation.

Hitler had more grandiose plans for eastern Europe, which he started to implement during the war. After defeating Poland he annexed the Corridor, Silesia and a small section of territory bordering on East Prussia. Rump-Poland (now called the General Government of the Occupied Polish Territories) was handed over to a civilian German administration under the notorious Dr Hans Frank. Then, when the Soviet Union was invaded in 1941, Bialystok province was annexed outright and two vast territories, Ostland and the Ukraine, were created and ruled by civilian commissariats, while two further regions, Muscovy and the Caucasus, were planned but owing to the defeat of the German forces were never set up.

All the bitter rivalries and contradictions of the Nazi regime were exported to the occupied areas, and consequently German occupation policy was seriously undermined by the unending series of feuds and power struggles among the German administrators [**doc. 16**]. Although, for example, the German military administration in occupied France was responsible for supervising the running of the zone, there was nevertheless the inevitable 'bewildering overlap of authority' (**126**(2), p. 203) between the army, the Armistice Commission which was set up to deal with economic problems, and the German Foreign Office Delegation. There was also considerable friction between the SS* and the military authorities when, in early 1942, a senior SS official was sent to watch over both the German and French police forces operating in the Occupied Zone.

In Poland Hans Frank (**56**) may have been called a 'megalomaniac Pasha' (**126**(2), p. 85) by his military colleagues, but in fact his power was far from absolute. The army, Göring, as Plenipotentiary of the Four Year Plan, and the Reich Defence Council all had the right to intervene in Polish affairs and issue decrees to protect their particular spheres of interest. Frank's greatest rival was Himmler, who as head of the security forces and of the Reich Commissariat for the Strengthening of the German Race (RKFDV*), which was responsible for implementing the key policy of German resettlement, was in a powerful position to challenge him. Himmler initially created the greatest difficulties for Frank by using occupied Poland as a dumping ground for Poles, Gypsies and Jews expelled from the newly annexed territories, and in 1942–43 his attempts to Germanise the Lublin area by settling ethnic Germans caused havoc by seriously disrupting local agriculture and driving many of the Polish peasants over to the partisans [**doc. 16**].

There was a similar pattern of conflict in the Ukraine and Ostland. Rosenberg (**56**) was appointed head of the Reich Ministry for the East, but far from enjoying the powers of a viceroy he was unable to secure acceptance for his policies for winning over minority nationalities in the Soviet Union. He repeatedly and ineffectually clashed with the generals, Himmler and Göring, who all pursued quasi-independent and contradictory policies. Dallin has shown that the chaos which marked German rule in the Soviet Union arose because 'the basic contradiction between long-range objectives and immediate demands was never reconciled' (**113**, p. 664). Thus, 'at the very moment when some pressed for the utmost use of labour in eastern agriculture, others forcibly transported farm hands to work in the Reich. While the Army sought to enrol Soviet prisoners as troops, German factories pressed for their use in labour' (**113**, p. 664). The disastrous effect of these contradictory policies was further exacerbated by the acute shortage of efficient German administrators and by the sheer size of the Russian commissariats.

Hitler's fundamental aim in both eastern and western Europe was 'to provide the master race with land for settlement and resources for exploitation' (**139**, p. 111). However, in western Europe German intentions were to a certain extent veiled by the veneer of idealistic talk about a united anti-Bolshevik Europe in which there would be, in the words of Otto Dietrich, Germany's press chief, 'equal chances for all' (**139**, p. 140). The meeting of the leaders of the Anti-Comintern Pact in Berlin in 1941 was described as 'the first European Congress', and even a 'Song of Europe' was written to celebrate it. Paradoxically, a more practical expression to European unity was given by Himmler, who at first recruited only Germanic volunteers for the *Waffen SS*, but then, as the German need for manpower grew, recruited a veritable 'United Nations' of peoples: Frenchmen, Ukrainians and even a few Indians were to be found in their ranks. Himmler also had little difficulty in recruiting a 'Black International' (**146**) drawn from a wide range of European peoples to guard the concentration camps. In the autumn of 1940 Hitler could have won over a considerable body of European opinion for a united Europe under the leadership of Germany had he been prepared to make any concessions, but his actions made it brutally clear that he was only interested in 'the defences and security of [Germany's] life interests' (**139**, p. 141).

Hitler's primary aim in eastern Europe was to found a series of new German colonies (**122**). In the former Polish territory which had been annexed by the Reich in 1939 a start was made in resettling German refugees from the Baltic states and eastern Poland, which had reverted to Russian rule in 1939–40. By 1943 the RKFDV* had expelled about a million Jews and Poles and brought in roughly the equivalent number of ethnic Germans, of whom only about half were settled on the land. The remainder spent the war in refugee camps. Hitler wished to reduce the Polish population to a semi-illiterate mass whose main function would be to serve the interests of Greater Germany, and to allow the economy to deteriorate into what he called 'Polish chaos' (**126**(2), p. 86).

In the Soviet Union Hitler's plans were far more ambitious. Initially he intended only to annex the Baltic states, former Austrian Galicia and the Crimea, as well as the lands inhabited by the Volga Germans, and he envisaged the eventual settlement of a hundred million Germans in western Russia. Both Himmler and Rosenberg produced a series of draft colonisation plans, and in May 1942 the Planning Office of the RKFDV* completed the notorious General Plan East, which envisaged a preliminary settlement of the Ukraine and Volga regions with a network of frontier marches or settlements populated by tough SS* war veterans who would act as soldier-settlers and would be defended from native revolts by mobile defence forces. The plan was a long-term one and envisaged only about three and a half million settlers at the end of the first twenty-five years. A beginning was actually made at Hegewald in the Ukraine in November 1942. Seven villages were cleared of their population and ethnic Germans were moved in from Volhynia, but the defeat at Stalingrad forced Hitler to abandon any further settlement plans (**113**, **122**), and belatedly in 1944 he even appeared to reverse his original policy of destroying the Russian state when he allowed General Vlasov, the captured Red Army general, to set up the Committee for the Liberation of the Peoples of Russia and to organise a congress at Prague where a constitution for a new non-Bolshevik federal Russia was unveiled (**113**). However, such concessions, coming after three years of Nazi atrocities and sporadic attempts by Rosenberg to encourage separatism among the minority peoples, were both too little and too late.

In other areas the Germans were eventually forced by sheer economic and military pressure to adopt a more pragmatic approach. In the first two years of the war the Germans had adopted a crude policy of 'smash and grab' (**139**, p. 116) towards the economies of the occupied territories. Both in Poland and the Soviet Union the initial policy was to send back anything of value to the Reich, and even in France, where plundering was less blatant, initially 250 train-loads of arms and war materials were transported across the frontier. However, the failure of the *Blitzkrieg** in the winter of 1941–42 compelled the Germans to make belated economic concessions to the Russians. In February 1942 the New Agrarian Order was introduced, which turned the Soviet collective farms into communal farms owned by the peasants themselves, and in June 1943 further concessions consolidated the peasants' legal rights to any lands they had gained since 1941 (**113**). The growing demand for munitions persuaded Hitler to abandon his original policy of de-industrialising the Soviet Union. By July 1942 steps had been taken to rebuild industry in the Donets Basin, but, before the Germans were driven out by the Red Army, production had only reached 10 per cent of its pre-war level. Under pressure of military and economic needs Hitler even began to tolerate a 'modest industrial build up' in Poland (**139**, p. 118).

In western Europe the Nazis were more willing to harness local industry to the needs of the German war economy. No attempts were made to dismantle Belgian or Dutch industry, and relatively subtle and semi-legal ploys were used to exploit the French economy and ensure German control of key industries. An arbitrary exchange rate was fixed, and clearing accounts were established in Berlin which enabled the Germans to defer payment for French material until after the war. With government backing German banks attempted, with some success, to gain control of the French investment banks, and mixed Franco-German companies were set up in which the Germans held a majority of shares. Despite its vastly greater size, Russia's economic contribution to the German war effort was only one-seventh of the French (**22**).

The most hated and politically counter-productive aspect of Hitler's economic exploitation of Europe was the conscription of foreign labour to work in Germany. By the end of 1941 nearly four million foreigners – both civilians and prisoners of war – were employed in Germany. In 1942, when it became clear that the war was not going to be quickly over, Fritz Sauckel was appointed to head the newly created Office of Labour Allocation, and ruthlessly combed through German-occupied Europe in search of workers. Up to 1942 racial prejudice had prevented Hitler from utilising the huge reservoirs of Soviet manpower in the prisoner-of-war camps where hundreds of thousands were allowed to die in the winter of 1941–2 [**doc. 15**], but by the following summer 'ideological distaste could no longer stand in the way of necessity' (**139**, p. 121) and in mid-1943 there were one and a half million Russian workers in Germany. A year later there were altogether seven million foreigners of both sexes employed in German industry.

In the autumn of 1943 Albert Speer, the German Armaments Minister, took a significant step towards building an integrated European economy (**17, 126**(2)). He negotiated an agreement with Jean Bichelonne, the Vichy Minister for Industrial Production, whereby French industry would take over the production of consumer goods for the German market and so enable German factories to concentrate on war production. It was arranged that the French would meet the production quotas set by Berlin in exchange for the ending of labour conscription. However, as was frequently the case in the Third Reich, the clash of personal rivalries and contradictory plans prevented any consistent policy emerging. Sauckel protested vigorously and in the end persuaded Hitler to authorise a continuation of labour conscription in France.

Hitler's short-lived European empire was an improvised structure in which pragmatic and ideological policies vied with each other. Pressure of events drove Hitler haltingly towards adopting policies which, if wholeheartedly implemented in 1939–41, could perhaps have enabled him to win the war.

13 The Holocaust

The unbelievable cruelty of the Holocaust renders it a particularly difficult subject for the historian to analyse dispassionately. The structuralist view (**151, 159, 156**), that the Holocaust was as much a consequence of muddle and improvisation as of clear planning, can all too easily degenerate into an apologia for Hitler and the Nazi regime. Dawidowicz, for instance, accuses the structuralists of a 'mechanistic interpretation' of Nazi Germany, which eliminates personal blame (**152**, Intro.). On the other hand, the intentionalists' understandable emphasis on the unique horror of the Holocaust can also inhibit legitimate attempts by historians to subject it to a rational analysis. The very use of the word 'holocaust', the dictionary definition of which is 'a sacrifice totally consumed by fire or a burnt offering', reflects, according to Marrus, 'an urge not only to distinguish this massacre from all others but also to register the ethereal quality of this terrible episode, its removal from customary discourse' (**158**, p. 115). Undoubtedly one of the most difficult problems facing historians of the Third Reich is to pin-point when and by whom the decision was taken to murder the Jews. Their task is made more difficult by the fact that there is no clear documentary link between Hitler and the destruction of the Jews in the death camps. On the whole, intentionalist historians argue that the decision was taken once war broke out in September 1939. John Fox, for example, believes that 'the main purpose and objective of Hitler's war in Europe from 1939 to 1945 was to destroy utterly and totally Russian Jewry followed in turn by European Jewry' (**154**, p. 3). The structuralists are, however, less certain. Many have been struck by how 'evolutionary' or 'improvised' (**158**, p. 125) Nazi anti-Jewish policy in practice was.

The large-scale settlement plans involving the movement of millions of people and the systematic attempt to destroy the Russian and Polish elites provided the context in which the murder of nearly six million Jews took place. The conquest of Poland put between two and three million Jews into Hitler's power, while there were a further half million in occupied territory in western Europe and some three million in Russia. In the winter of 1939–40 the new Reich Security Main Office (RSHA) under the control of Heydrich was given a free hand to create Jewish 'reservations' and ghettos in occupied Poland. There the Jews in those Polish territories that were about to be annexed to the Reich were to be 'resettled'. However, the sheer scale of the logistical problems involved in resettling hundreds of thousands of people in wartime forced Göring, who still had overall responsibility for the Jewish question, to call a halt to the resettlement programme in March 1940 (8(III)).

Emigration continued to remain official policy at least up to June 1941, but during this period only about 71,500 Jews managed to leave Reich territory with the official permission of the Nazi government. After the fall of France there momentarily appeared to be a possibility of resettling the European Jewish population in the French colony of Madagascar, but the continuation of hostilities with Britain and Hitler's reluctance to alienate Vichy France (see above, p. 63) ensured that until Germany had won the war this scheme was not viable (8(III)). Does the Madagascar Plan then indicate that Hitler had not initially planned to exterminate the Jews? Did later unforeseen events force this action upon him and upon those whom he had made responsible for solving the Jewish 'problem'? Essentially, it is important to grasp that plans for 'resettlement' in Madgascar, or later in Siberia, were not really an alternative to extermination. One German historian, Hermann Graml, has convincingly argued that the Nazi authorities assumed that the great majority of Jews would anyway die from disease on Madgascar and that consequently mass murder would be 'given the appearance of a natural process' (155, p. 82). In this context it is also worth stressing that Philipp Bouhler, who had been in charge of the euthanasia programme in Germany (see p. 79), had been tipped as the first governor of Madagascar (152).

Given, then, that Germany remained at war with Britain, the RSHA in the winter of 1940–41 had little option but to revert to its original plan of concentrating the Jews in ghettos in eastern Poland. This too ran into insuperable logistical problems as it coincided with the military build-up in preparation for the invasion of Russia. Nevertheless, Hitler was unwilling to stop the deportation programme, although in practice the lack of sufficient transport facilities had conspired to slow it down. In April 1941 he specifically vetoed suggestions from Göring that the Jews in

Reich territory should be employed in the local war industries [**doc. 11b**].

The real turning point in Nazi policy towards the Jews came with the invasion of Soviet Russia in June 1941. Not only did this bring some three million more Jews under German control, but the whole campaign was an overtly ideological struggle fought against Bolshevism, which to the Nazis was merely another manifestation of the Jewish bid for world power [**doc. 11a**]. Hitler himself made clear to his generals on 30 March 1941 that they were about to embark upon 'a war of extermination' (**8**(III), p. 1086). The German High Command then issued the notorious Commissar Order whereby all captured Red Army political officers were to be shot. On Hitler's specific orders special SS* *Einsatzgruppen*, or task forces, were given the job of 'mopping up' behind the lines of the invading German army. Although they were supposed only to execute Communist officials and 'Jews in service of the state' (**8**(III), p. 1091), in fact by the spring of 1942 well over a million Jews, who had nothing to do with the Communist Party, had been murdered (**159**).

Undoubtedly, massacres on this scale marked a new and more deadly stage in Nazi policy. However, historians do not agree on when and how the actual decision was taken to begin the Holocaust or systematic extermination of European Jewry. On 31 July 1941 Heydrich was ordered by Göring to draw up a detailed plan 'for bringing about a complete solution of the Jewish question within the German sphere of Europe' (**8**(III), p. 1104). Göring may well have intended Heydrich to draw up a blueprint for total extermination of European Jewry, but the wording of the document is ambiguous. The structuralists argue that at this stage the assumption in Berlin was still that the war would soon be over and the Jews would be 'resettled' in Madagascar or perhaps more likely Siberia. They argue that it was the unexpected success of the Red Army in December 1941 which was the crucial factor leading to the Holocaust (**151, 156, 159**). Not only did the continuation of the war make Siberia inaccessible to the Nazis, but the constant need to keep the German armies supplied also created enormous logistical problems in Poland and occupied Russia, which could only be made worse by the deportation of further Jews into the area. Arguably, then, a large-scale programme for liquidating the Jews was, in Broszat's words, a '"way out" of a blind alley into which the National Socialists had manoeuvred themselves' (**151**, p. 405). The intentionalists vehemently criticise the implications of

Broszat's argument that the Holocaust was in effect an accidental consequence of the military situation in eastern Europe. Dawidowicz, for instance, argues that Hitler 'implemented his plan in stages, seizing whatever opportunities offered themselves to advance its execution' (**152**, Intro.). This stress on the combination of opportunism and planning in Hitler's thinking is familiar and has already been noted by Bullock in relation to his foreign policy (see p. 51 above). It was certainly the way that Hitler proceeded, but then, as has already been emphasised, the lack of documents linking Hitler directly to key decisions on the Holocaust makes it much more difficult for historians to trace his precise role in these terrible events. Nevertheless, by late 1941 there were so many Nazi initiatives aiming at the eventual extermination of the Jews that it is very probable that 'a green light was coming from the highest level' (**8**(III), p. 1136). At the very least, it must have been abundantly clear to Hitler's followers and officials that he favoured such policies. Arguably, this alone was sufficient to guarantee that they would compete with one another to ensure their implementation (**156, 158, 159**).

In January 1942 an attempt was made at the Wannsee Conference in Berlin to coordinate these various initiatives. Details were worked out for the wholesale conscription of Jews into labour gangs in eastern Europe, where it was chillingly assumed that 'a large number will drop out through natural elimination'. The remainder would then be 'dealt with accordingly' (**8**(III), p. 1131). Extermination camps were built in 1942 at Belzec, Sobibor and Treblinka, and a year later two more death camps were opened at Maydanek and Auschwitz. By 1945 nearly six million Jews had been murdered.

Mommsen has argued that 'the psychological bridge between the emigration and reservation "solutions" and the Holocaust itself was created by the fiction of *Arbeitseinsatz*' or labour mobilization' (**159**, p. 124). Was the Holocaust inevitable once war broke out in 1939? It is probable, as the structuralists stress, that the exact form it took was largely dictated by events in eastern Europe. The intentionalists are nevertheless correct in stressing Hitler's absolute determination to rid the European states of their Jewish citizens; and that process would not have been gentle. In the course of 'resettlement' in Madagascar or Siberia millions of Jews would almost certainly have died from disease or starvation – or have been murdered.

Part Five: The Third Reich at War, 1939–45

14 The Home Front

Despite momentary crises of confidence Hitler's personal ascendancy in Germany remained virtually unchallenged until his suicide in April 1945 [**doc. 17**]. In September 1939 he withdrew from the public eye and immersed himself in the problems of the war, and two years later, in November 1941, when he assumed direct responsibility for military operations, he isolated himself for most of the time in his bleak East Prussian headquarters at the Wolfsschanze. Even in 1943, which was a year of multiple defeats, Hitler only made three public speeches (**73**(II)). During the last four months of the war he was cut off from all reality in the Berlin bunker and directed the war 'by somnambulist decisions' (**149**, p. 17).

With Hitler distracted by the military aspect of the war, the government of the Reich became even more of a battlefield for contending factions than it had been before the war (**74**, **73**(II), chs 5–7). On 30 August 1939 the Reich Defence Council was set up under Göring, but it failed to develop into a real war cabinet and was consequently unable to coordinate the various ministries and party agencies (**54**). In the war years the power and influence of the Nazi Party significantly increased. Both Himmler and the SS* and Bormann and the Party Chancellery, which was responsible for coordinating party policy, made considerable inroads on the authority of the state. The SS not only continued to develop into a 'collateral state' but began to undermine and even dissolve the existing state institutions (**56**, p. 180). In the occupied areas it was awarded the key responsibility for organising the resettlement of ethnic Germans, and the control and administration of the concentration camps gave it access to a large pool of labour which could be used exclusively in its industrial undertakings (**54**, **75**). By the end of the war the economic empire of the SS comprised about 150 firms organised together into one large trust, the *Deutsche Wirtschaftsbetriebe GmbH*, the activities of which ranged from quarrying, mining and the production of foodstuffs and mineral waters to the manufacture of armaments and textiles. The economic thinking of the SS was fundamentally anti-capitalist, and there is some evidence to suggest that Himmler hoped in the long term to undermine German capitalism (**96**).

Besides controlling the Gestapo* and running its own security service (the SD* or *Sicherheitsdienst*), which spied with impunity on top Nazi functionaries, the SS* was also given responsibility for military intelligence and for guarding prisoners of war in 1944. In the last two years of the war the *Waffen SS* was expanded up to a point where it nominally consisted of 35 divisions. Himmler occupied an increasing number of important posts over the same period. He was appointed Reich Minister of the Interior in 1943, Commander of the Reserve Army in 1944, and then in quick succession Commander-in-Chief of the Rhine Army Group in December 1944 and of the Vistula Army Group in January 1945. But paradoxically, while Himmler's power reached unprecedented heights in the Reich, his influence on Hitler was quietly and doggedly undermined by Bormann, who remained at Hitler's side throughout the war (**56**).

The war also presented the Nazi Party with numerous opportunities to extend its growth and influence at both central and local level. The majority of the Gauleiters* were appointed Reich Defence Commissioners in September 1939, and in 1943 were authorised to take complete charge of the civil authorities within their *Gaue** in the event of an invasion. In this role they behaved like barons in a period of feudal anarchy. They jealously hoarded labour so that they could keep industry in their own *Gaue* functioning, and in the last six months of the war did not hesitate to commandeer for local use vital coal trains *en route* to supply industry elsewhere (**17**).

At the start of the war the party was assigned the task of maintaining the morale of the civilian population. The military successes in Poland and western Europe re-awoke the party's ambition to engineer the social and racial revolution which had been denied it in the 1930s. There were therefore renewed attacks on the Church and attempts to plant party cells in the civil service and to attach political commissars to the army. Hitler was, however, still wary of any radical reform which could disturb the unity of the Reich. The euthanasia programme, for example, which between January 1940 and August 1941 caused the murder of some 70,000 handicapped people, had to be modified and made more secretive because of mounting public hostility (**8**(III), **83**, **89**).

In the occupied territories the party enjoyed unprecedented opportunities to assert its authority. The Reich Commissioners there were theoretically state officials, but were in reality party functionaries, many of whom were Gauleiters*. Although the SS* and the party were frequently rivals, they both cooperated whole-heartedly in the destruction of the Jews.

After Hess's flight to Scotland in May 1941 Bormann became the head of the Party Chancellery and gave fresh impetus to the encroachment of the party on both German society and the state (**73**(II)). Bormann was a formidable bureaucrat who exploited his position, which was further enhanced by his appointment as Hitler's secretary in 1943, to control access to Hitler. By early 1945 the Party Chancellery had eclipsed the Reich Chancellery, which had been the traditional channel through which government business reached Hitler. The party tightened its grip on education in September 1941 by insisting that political reliability rather than academic success should be the key to entering teacher training colleges. In April 1942 the top officials at the Ministry of Justice were replaced by more pliant candidates, and the party increas-ingly interfered in the actual course of justice by indicating to judges beforehand what their verdicts should be. Bormann also succeeded in taking a significant step in the 'partification' of the civil service by installing Hans von Helm, an ardent advocate of party control, as personnel director in the Ministry of the Interior. Then in September 1944 Hitler created the *Volkssturm**, which was in effect a party militia organised on the territorial basis of the *Gaue**. Orlow has aptly described the activities of the Party Chancellery as a 'cancer' which 'from the darkness of the East Prussian forests and later from the bunker of the Reich Chancellery...directed...the subversion of what remained of the German *Rechtsstaat** and orderly lines of communication' (**73**(II), p. 478).

It is surprising that a country with such a chaotic system of government was capable of waging a major war for nearly six years, but then the party never quite succeeded in erasing the Prussian traditions of excellence in the civil service and army. The brilliant military successes of 1939–41 also saved the Hitler regime from initially having to face up to the demanding realities of total war. Milward has described the *Blitzkrieg** as a 'system of warfare best suited to the character and institutions of Hitler's Germany' (**96**, p. 31), as it did not entail full mobilisation of all economic resources, thereby putting the civilian population under strain at a time when it was far from convinced of the need for war. This interpretation under-estimates the extent of Germany's economic mobilisation and Hitler's determination to prepare Germany for a major and, if necessary, lengthy conflict with a coalition of Great Powers (**98, 99**). Nevertheless, the victories of 1940–41 did take considerable psychological pressure off the German people. Hitler and the Gauleiters* were terrified of a recurrence of the revolution of 1918, and thus almost up to the end of the war whenever a question of civilian morale clashed with the needs of the war economy, morale won. In September 1939, for example, when an attempt to cut workers' wages and scrap various bonus schemes met with considerable opposition, the regime hastily retreated and restored bonuses for Sunday and night work and put back wage rates to their pre-war levels, although it simultaneously introduced a wages freeze and lowered the exemption rate of income tax as a face-saver. Similarly, a few months later swingeing increases in income tax were vetoed in favour of less painful fiscal means for fear of alienating public opinion (**94, 98**).

The Nazi regime also ensured that the German population was at least adequately fed and therefore not driven to desperation by hunger (**87, 89**). In September 1939 there were considerable grain reserves in Germany, but it was still necessary to introduce strict food rationing. Up to 1944 average consumers received rations which were between 7 and 15 per cent above the minimum calorific standard, but in the last year of the war these were drastically cut. Workers in heavy industry were guaranteed adequate rations, which often proved to be more generous than their peacetime diets. The German population benefited surprisingly little from Hitler's conquests, as the Allied blockade deprived western European agriculture of imported fodder and fertilisers and the Ukrainian harvests were used exclusively for feeding the army (**87**).

Despite the absence of a free press, the regime was able to gain a clear picture of the state of civilian morale through the regular and comprehensive reports compiled by the SD*. Until the victories of 1940 the German population remained unenthusiastic about the war and by December 1940 the temporary euphoria of the summer had settled down into what Goebbels described as 'slight depression' (**5**, p. 107) [**doc. 18a**]. The Russian campaign, the entry of America into the war, and particularly the disaster at Stalingrad, gravely impaired public morale. Momentarily Goebbels, the Reich Propaganda Minister, rallied the German people in February 1943 with a frank appeal for total war (**63**), but the remorseless bombing and further defeats in Africa, the Soviet Union and Italy combined to depress morale still further (**105**) [**doc. 18b**].

Yet at the same time the impressive rise in armaments production showed that the German population was by no means ready to surrender [**doc. 19**]. Allied bombing and demands for unconditional surrender, as well as the dire threats of de-industrialising Germany made in the Morgenthau Plan, which Speer described as 'made to order for Hitler and the party' (**17**, p. 433), convinced the German public that there was no option but total war. The ever-present threat of the Gestapo* helped, of course, to keep the population docile, but until the end of the war there was a surprising residue of personal loyalty to Hitler, although the party itself was becoming increasingly unpopular (**72**) [**doc. 17**].

The Nazi war machine could not have functioned without the efforts of Fritz Todt and Albert Speer (**17**, **96**, **98**). Todt was appointed Minister for Armaments and Munitions in March 1940 and laid the foundations for 'a strong indirect control by a civil ministry of armaments production' (**96**, p. 61) by setting up a series of committees, the chairmen of which he himself appointed for the most part from industry. By December 1941 it was clear that the *Blitzkrieg** had failed and that Germany would now drastically have to rationalise its armament production. The enormous increase in munitions and equipment which *Führer*-command 'Armament 1942' ultimately brought about was not so much the product of increased investment in the war, but rather the belated adoption of more efficient techniques of mass production and better organisation (**98**). These orders marked the final break with the *Blitzkrieg* economy. Todt was killed in an air crash in February 1942 and was replaced by Speer, who built on the foundations already laid by his predecessor. In April 1942 he successfully persuaded Hitler to create the Central Planning Board, which was to organise the allocation of raw materials to each sector of the economy. Speer was also ultimately successful in wresting from the army and navy their jealously guarded prerogative of designing their own weapons. Speer's efforts were rewarded by a steady increase in armaments production which, despite heavy Allied bombing, reached its peak in 1943–44 [**doc. 19**].

Speer owed much of his success to his good relations with Hitler, which 'enabled him to chop into tiny pieces the red tape' which had prevented the development of a really efficient armaments programme in the 1930s (**96**, p. 86). However, even Speer's ministry suffered from the endemic faults in the Nazi system, and in Craig's words he was ultimately 'denied the right to go beyond the limit of what rationalization could accomplish' (**22**, p. 734). He was hampered by both the autonomy of the Gauleiters* and the independence of the SS*, the considerable economic resources of which were beyond his grasp. Hitler's reluctance to agree to the industrial conscription of all available women exacerbated the labour shortages which Sauckel, the Plenipotentiary-General for Labour, only temporarily alleviated with foreign labour. In January 1943 Hitler at last agreed in principle to female conscription, but in practice only about 900,000 women were called up. Even at this date there were still over a million women employed as domestic servants (**90**). Ultimately, however, the logic of total war overrode Nazi scruples about employing female labour. By the end of the war some 51 per cent of the German work force was female (**98**).

15   The End of the Third Reich

By the autumn of 1944 it was obvious 'to all but fanatics [that] the war was economically lost' (**96**, p. 163). Allied bombing had reduced oil supplies to a dangerously low level and disrupted transport facilities throughout the Reich, thereby dislocating the supply of coal, steel and other vital raw materials to the factories. In October the acute shortage of labour was made worse by the creation of the *Volkssturm**, which absorbed a large number of men who would have been better employed making armaments. The loss of the occupied territories and the increasing reluctance of the neutrals to sell Germany raw materials also worsened the already chronic economic difficulties and shortages. Once the Russians, who had, of course, of all the Allies done the most to destroy the German army, occupied the industrial areas of Silesia in January and the British the Ruhr in April 1945 the German war economy could no longer function.

In December 1944 Hitler gambled heavily on driving a wedge between the British and American forces in the west by striking unexpectedly through the Ardennes. When he failed, he retreated to his bunker in Berlin. He had become a physical wreck quite incapable of recognising political and military realities (**149**). He placed a pathetic reliance on the effectiveness of secret weapons and on the inevitability of a rupture between the United States and the Soviet Union. His feelings for the German people who had apparently not been worthy of him turned to bitter nihilistic scorn, and he planned to drag them into the abyss after him. He urged Speer to prepare a scorched earth policy which would leave Germany a desert for the invading allies. Hitler may well have been envisaging the creation of a legend of heroism for some future German warlord (**149**), but as Speer later observed, 'Hitler himself, measured by the standards of his own political programme, was deliberately committing high treason against his own people' (**17**, p. 429).

While Hitler's nihilism met with little support in Germany in early 1945, there was no German revolution as in November 1918.

It is true that Speer, with considerable bravery and skill, circumvented or defied Hitler's orders to destroy factories and power stations, but although at one juncture he seriously considered gassing Hitler and his 'court' in the bunker, in the final analysis he could not bring himself to betray his *Führer* (**17**). There is much truth in Trevor-Roper's observation that 'Hitler still remained, in the universal chaos he had caused, the sole master whose orders were implicitly obeyed' (**149**, p. 183). Himmler only dared ask the Swedes to mediate with the western powers when he mistakenly thought that Hitler was dead.

Hitler shot himself in the bunker, which was already under Russian artillery fire, on 29 April 1945, after nominating Admiral Doenitz as his successor (**149**). Both Göring and Himmler had been discredited because they had dared to take independent action in the mistaken belief that Hitler had either abdicated or died. Doenitz set up his government in Flensburg in Schleswig-Holstein, where, despite his attempts to assert the continuity of German history since 1871, it was painfully obvious that his brief regime was 'only the last stage of the Third Reich, nothing more' (**17**, p. 500). The government functioned in a vacuum, strangely ignored by the British occupying forces until its members were arrested on 23 May 1945.

Part Six: Assessment

16   The German Opposition to Hitler

In 1945, when the full horrors of the concentration camps and the 'final solution' became known, it was understandable for Allied observers to belittle the German opposition, especially since its members appeared, as Taylor caustically expressed it, to 'resolve to put their fine principles into action only when the Anglo-American armies had established themselves in Normandy and the Red Army was at the gates of Warsaw' (**34**, p. 262). However, over the ensuing decades it has become clearer that there was an extensive, though uncoordinated, opposition to Hitler and that it functioned in conditions of exceptional difficulty and danger. In 1939, according to Gestapo statistics, there were 27,367 German political prisoners and between 1933 and 1939 a total of 112,432 German citizens had been sentenced for political offences (**144**).

The German opposition (**141, 142, 144, 146**) existed in uniquely difficult conditions. Unlike the resistance movements in German-occupied Europe, it had to work among a population which by and large accepted Hitler with varying degrees of enthusiasm, and once war started many Germans who had reservations about Hitler regarded its activities as treasonable. It also lacked any reliable base within Germany or, with the exception of the Communists whose umbilical cord led to Moscow, the firm support of a friendly power abroad. The Churches, the army, the unions, the Pope, the western powers and even Stalin all initially attempted to bargain with Hitler, thereby making it doubly difficult for a root-and-branch opposition to flourish. The Nazi security system was also highly effective, and in wartime the population was placed under a close surveillance which uncovered opposition network after network. Internally Hitler could only be overthrown by either a popular uprising – which, once organised labour movements had been broken, was hardly a viable proposition – a palace revolution engineered by one of his lieutenants, or a military coup. In fact only the third option was at all practical in the circumstances of the Third Reich.

Only a small number of exceptionally brave people joined the active opposition. Many more who hated the Third Reich formed what Rothfels called the 'silent opposition' (**146**, p. 29), which defied Hitler unobtrusively by hiding Jews [**doc. 20**], listening to the BBC, reading banned literature or even coining anti-Nazi jokes [**doc. 18(b)**]. Some writers and intellectuals simply withdrew from public life and attempted to avoid contact with the regime (a process known as internal emigration), while others used learned articles or analyses of past tyrannies as vehicles for obliquely criticising the Nazi regime (**22**). Clearly, however, this was fundamentally ineffective and could hardly bring down Hitler, even though it might succeed in saving some of his victims from the concentration camp or the gas chamber.

The Lutheran and Roman Catholic Churches should have been in the vanguard of the opposition to Hitler, but to their shame they never committed themselves to total war against Nazism. Thanks to Martin Niemöller and the several thousand priests who formed the breakaway Confessional Church, the Lutheran Church defeated attempts to absorb it into the new *Reichskirche**, but this major victory by no means implied a political or moral opposition to Hitler. Like the army, the Lutheran Church was intent primarily on preserving its independence rather than becoming 'the spearhead of political opposition to the Nazis' (**85**, p. 84). Nevertheless, a considerable number of Lutheran priests did openly criticise Hitler, as is testified by the death of nearly 400 in Buchenwald and the career of Dietrich Bonhoeffer, who categorically described Hitler as the Anti-Christ to be rooted out, and became a major figure in the German opposition until he was arrested in 1943.

The Pope sought to preserve the Roman Catholic Church by coming to terms with Hitler in the Concordat of July 1933, which had the effect of blunting the opposition of Roman Catholic priests in Germany towards the Nazis and of reconciling their flocks to the new regime. As with the Lutheran Church, only in certain limited spheres did the Roman Catholics confront the Nazis (**23**, **144**). A stubborn battle was, for example, fought to prevent the absorption of Catholic youth groups into the Hitler youth. In 1937 the Pope went as far as issuing the famous Encyclical, 'With Burning Concern', which condemned Hitler's violations of the Concordat and his racial policy, but tragically this remained an exception to the general policy of tolerating the regime. However, as in the Lutheran Church, there were a number of priests who openly spoke out against Hitler and his policies. It was, for example, largely due to Count Galen, the Bishop of

Münster, that the public was informed of Hitler's euthanasia programme in 1941, while the Jesuit, Father Alfred Delp, was a member of the Kreisau Circle before he was arrested and executed.

Initially Hitler's most implacable opponents were found on the Left, but the destruction of the political parties and the trade unions deprived them of their power bases and forced them to operate from underground or abroad. The SPD*, for example, established party headquarters first in Prague and then in Paris, and up to 1939 managed to smuggle illegal literature across the frontiers (**144, 146**). SPD and trade-union cells were from time to time established in factories and large cities but were so quickly broken up by the Gestapo* that the party executive in Prague decided in 1937 to concentrate on merely maintaining communications with its supporters in the Reich so that after the collapse of the Hitler regime there would at least exist a nucleus for a future SPD. As it was painfully clear that neither the SPD nor the unions could effectively oppose Hitler, several prominent SPD politicians in the underground, such as Wilhelm Leuschner, Julius Leber and Carlo Mierendorff, began to look to the army as the only workable opposition against Hitler and consequently contacted the conservative opposition groups and the disaffected generals.

The history of the Communist contribution to the German opposition was distorted by the Cold War (**141, 144**). The East Germans exaggerated its importance, while the West Germans initially minimised or ignored it. The Communists were more skilled than the SPD* in adapting their organisations to underground activities, and despite repeated Gestapo* raids and heavy losses Communist cells were never completely eliminated. The orthodox German Communists accepted without debate the party line as laid down in Moscow, where the German Central Committee in exile functioned. Initially the Communists concentrated on building up their membership in preparation for the proletarian revolution, but by 1935, in obedience to Stalin's instructions, they had belatedly begun to negotiate with the SPD for a united front against Fascism, which after the years of mistrust and hostility between the two parties proved impossible to form. During the period of the Nazi-Soviet Pact the KPD* was instructed to support Stalin's foreign policy but to oppose Hitler within Germany. In June 1941 Hitler's attack gave fresh impetus to the formation of Communist underground groups such as those set up by Bernhard Bästlein and Franz Jakob in Hamburg or Robert Uhrig and Anton

Saefkow in Berlin, all of which acted from time to time independently of the Moscow party line. Perhaps the most famous Communist group was the *Rote Kapelle* (Red Orchestra), which had cells both in industry and in several government ministries and supplied the Russians with much important information until it was uncovered by the Gestapo* in 1942.

Left-wing opposition was not confined to members of the two big parties. There were numerous small independent groups which, sickened by the divisions of the Left in the Weimar Republic, sought to bring about a realignment of left-wing forces in Germany (**141**). The *Roter Stosstrupp* (Red Assault Party), for example, called for a new party of the Left which would create a socialist society after the collapse of the Nazis, while another group, *Neu Beginnen* (New Start), aimed at reconciling the best elements in the KPD* and SPD* and at creating the basis for joint action against Hitler and cooperation in the reconstruction of society after the war. Craig has argued that the German resistance, 'despite its socialist and trade union component... never extended to the masses of the working class' (**22**, p. 667). It is undeniable that the Left failed to organise a mass movement, yet it is unfair to ignore the extent of anti-Nazi activity among the working classes. Carsten mentions 'the intense oppositional working class activity in Berlin' (**141**, Intro.) after 1933, and it is hard to ignore the fact that in 1936, for example, more than 11,000 people were arrested for assisting the SPD underground movement (**144**).

The potentially most effective resistance to Hitler was to be found in the National Conservative opposition, which was composed of prominent individuals or 'notables' who worked within the system to destroy Nazism. The leading members were all important men in the traditional German establishment. Erwin Planck, for example, had been Papen's former state secretary; Carl Goerdeler, Price Commissioner under both Papen and Hitler and Lord Mayor of Leipzig; Johannes Popitz, Prussian Finance Minister; Ulrich von Hassell, former German ambassador in Rome; and General Beck, Army Chief of Staff until 1938. Despite their isolation from the masses, these men had within their grasp the means of destroying Hitler, as they had close links with the army and under certain circumstances could win it over, although it would be necessary to wait until the Officer Corps was both disillusioned with Hitler and convinced that he was about to destroy Germany. Their first opportunity came in the summer of 1938, when the Officer Corps felt itself humiliated by Hitler's handling of the Blomberg-Fritsch affair and alarmed at his apparent intention to unleash a general European war for the sake of the Sudetenland. With the assistance of Generals Beck, Witzleben, Hammerstein and Halder a plan, which was to be implemented once the western powers had declared war, was drawn up to have Hitler arrested, martial law declared and a constituent assembly summoned, but the Munich settlement ironically destroyed what has been judged to have been a 'most promising attempt to overthrow Hitler' (**142**, p. 96).

There were frequent plans drawn up by members of the Conservative opposition to assassinate Hitler during the phoney war and, to their great credit, right through the period of his most spectacular victories (**142**). Paradoxically, once the tide turned against Germany in 1942 the problems facing the opposition were intensified, because Nazi Germany had so alienated world opinion that the western powers at any rate were determined to demand unconditional surrender and to brush aside feelers from the German opposition groups.

In 1940 the German opposition was strengthened by the formation of the Kreisau Circle (**146**), which was composed of a diverse group of anti-Nazis that met at Kreisau, the Silesian estate of Count Helmuth James von Moltke. The Circle became the intellectual powerhouse of the non-Communist opposition. Although Moltke attracted predominantly the younger generation of resisters, he also had a profound impact on Goerdeler and social democrats like Reichwein and Mierendorff. The Circle was smashed in January 1944 when Moltke was arrested by the Gestapo*. He was executed twelve months later.

The tragic failure in 1943 of the White Rose Group at Munich University, which was formed by a small group of students who called upon German youth to rise up and 'crush its torturers and to build a new spiritual Europe' (**144**, p. 168), and the risky but unsuccessful attempt by Popitz to weaken the Nazis by persuading Himmler to depose Hitler (**147**), emphasised afresh that the only effective way to bring down the regime was to employ the army against it. In 1943 plans to assassinate Hitler and stage a military *coup d'état* were given firm shape by Colonel Claus Schenk von Stauffenberg, who was working at the German Army Office in Berlin. Stauffenberg contacted activists on both the Right and the Left and became the key figure in planning 'Operation Valkyrie', the implementation of which would involve Hitler's assassination, the declaration of martial law, the setting up of a provisional government including Conservative, Centre, Social Democrat and non-party representatives, and immediate peace negotiations with the west. Although it is undeniable that the successful Allied landings in Normandy prompted Stauffenberg and the others to act, they were not simply fired by the desire to salvage what was left of Germany. They were also determined to prove to posterity that the German resistance dared, in Major-General von Tresckow's words, to stake 'its life on risking the decisive throw' (**146**, p. 79). The tragic history of 20 July 1944 is well known. In a sense it can of course be said to have failed because 'Colonel Brandt kicked Stauffenberg's briefcase to the wrong side of the oak support of the conference table' (**144**, p. 248), but it is also true that the bulk of the generals in Berlin dared not act decisively until they knew that Hitler was dead. If they had acted on the afternoon of 20 July the *coup d'état* could still have succeeded. Its failure led to the virtual elimination of the opposition, as Hitler arrested more than 7,000 people, 5,000 of whom had been executed by April 1945.

It has often been debated whether the Conservative opposition was fundamentally reactionary or in reality the herald of the 1949 Bonn Republic. The foreign policy of the Goerdeler-Hassell group was strongly nationalistic and, at any rate up to 1942, based on what Graml calls 'seductive visions of a German Reich of medieval proportions' and Prussian and conservative in character (**141**, p. 21). Under the influence of the Kreisau Circle Goerdeler did begin to write about a future federal Europe, but he never really abandoned his concept of Germany as an independent great power. The Kreisau Circle was more committed to a united European Federation, but even Moltke stipulated in 1943 that the Reich should remain 'the supreme leading power of the German People'.

The domestic policy of the Conservative opposition was fundamentally illiberal and anti-democratic. Mommsen has characterised the constitutional draft devised by Goerdeler as 'exceed[ing] Papen's wildest dreams' and the proposals of Popitz and Hassell as 'predominantly fascist' (**141**, p. 114). On the other hand Moltke and the Kreisau Circle devised a Christian-socialist programme which has been described as occupying a position between 'East and West'–that is, between Communism and Capitalism (**146**, p. 115). Yet Moltke can also be regarded as a radical conservative who fundamentally mistrusted liberalism and democracy. He wanted, for example, to limit direct elections to the local and district levels and would have given heads of families an additional vote for each child under twenty-one. It is, however, wise to accept Bracher's warning of the futility of stamping the Conservative German opposition with any label based on the few existing memoranda penned by individuals like Goerdeler or Moltke (**54**).

Whatever the politics of the German resistance groups were, it is clear that its members were men of great personal bravery who opposed Hitler primarily for moral reasons. Their tragedy was, as Ritter has observed, that they received no backing 'from either within or without' (**145**, p. 313). Those hundreds of thousands and perhaps millions of Germans who were secretly critical of the Third Reich behaved as the great majority of people of any nationality do in a dangerous and threatening situation and earned Sophie Scholl's rebuke, delivered at her trial before the People's Court in 1943: 'What we have written and said is in the mind of all of you, but you lack the courage to say it aloud' (**54**, p. 547).

17   Conclusion

The history of the Third Reich has been extensively analysed but controversy about its every aspect still shows no sign of abating. There is no real consensus, for instance, about Hitler's role as *Führer**, Nazi foreign or economic policy, the structure of the Nazi state or the sequence of events that led to the Holocaust. The cataclysmic end of the Third Reich and the appalling suffering it caused have tended to ensure that German history between the years 1933 and 1945 has been studied in isolation as a uniquely horrendous event in the history of mankind. In Germany, in a series of provocative books and articles which have triggered a major controversy among historians, Professor Nolte has attempted to put the history of Nazi Germany into perspective (**162, 164, 165**). Essentially, he argues that 'the essence of National Socialism' lay 'in its relation to Marxism and especially to Communism in the form this had taken on through the Bolshevik victory in the Russian Revolution' (**162, p. 28**). In other words, Nazi atrocities such as the Holocaust are only understandable as a reaction against the Bolshevik terror in the Russian civil war and Stalin's liquidation of the Kulaks (wealthy peasants) some ten years later. As with some of the structuralist historians in the Holocaust debate, Nolte comes perilously close to excusing Nazi atrocities, and it is this aspect of his work that has rightly incensed liberal opinion in Germany. Nevertheless, however painful it might be to non-Germans, Nolte has advanced a very strong case that if the Third Reich is to be understood, it has to be studied not only in relation to its times, but also within the context of the history of western civilisation over the last 200 years (**165**).

No simple formula suffices to explain Nazism. It was certainly a backlash against the destabilising process of the industrial revolution. It was arguably, in its concept of *Lebensraum**, also a late but particularly vicious expression of European imperialism, without the saving grace of the sense of responsibility and service that at times accompanied British and French colonial expansion, particularly in their later stages. Nazism cannot, however, be dismissed totally as a backward-looking, anachronistic movement. As Burleigh and Wippermann have shown, the novelty of the Nazi regime lay in its attempt to engineer 'an ideal future world, without "lesser races", without the sick, and without those who they decreed had no place in the "national community"'. The Third Reich was intended to become 'a racial rather than class society' (**83**, p. 306).

Hitler did not, of course, gain power because of his racial policies. Indeed, during the electoral campaigns of 1930–33 these were played down. His success in 1933 owed more to his image as a radical politician who would save Germany from economic misery and the threat of Communist-inspired anarchy. Once in power, the genuine achievement of the Nazi regime in creating full employment, combined perhaps with the 'verbal social revolution' and the terror apparatus of the Gestapo* and the SS*, ensured the workers' acquiescence. Based on the strongest economy in Europe, the Nazi dictatorship released an immense but eventually destructive burst of energy. The ultimate weakness of the regime, however, was that it gradually undermined the tradition of stable, orderly government within Germany and replaced it with a chaos of competing agencies dependent on a charismatic *Führer**. Hitler's own programme and the restless pressure of the party, and above all the SS, propelled Germany along a path of genocide and ever escalating territorial demands, which ultimately ended in catastrophic defeat.

Part Seven: Documents

Hitler as saviour

Speer describes why both he and his mother joined the Nazi Party in 1931. Speer, who was then a lecturer in architecture at the Berlin Institute of Technology, had just heard Hitler's speech to the students.

Here it seemed to me was hope. Here were new ideals, a new understanding, new tasks.... The perils of Communism which seemed inexorably on the way, could be checked, Hitler persuaded us, and instead of hopeless unemployment, Germany could move toward economic recovery. He had mentioned the Jewish problem only peripherally. But such remarks did not worry me, although I was not an anti-semite; rather I had Jewish friends from my school days and university days, like virtually everyone else.... It must have been during these months that my mother saw an S.A. parade in the streets of Heidelberg. The sight of discipline in a time of chaos, the impression of energy in an atmosphere of universal hopelessness, seems to have won her over also.

Speer (**17**), pp. 16–18.

Why the Centre Party voted for the Enabling Bill

Carl Bachem, who was the historian of the Centre Party, reflects on the wisdom of voting for the Enabling Bill.

In any case: as in 1919 we climbed calmly and deliberately into the Social Democrat boat, so in the same way, we were able to enter the boat of the National Socialists in 1933 and try to lend a hand with the steering. Between 1919 and 1933 this proved quite satis-factory: the Social Democrats, since they were not able to govern without the Centre, were unable to do anything particularly anti-religious or dubiously socialistic. Will it be possible to exercise a similarly sobering influence on the National Socialists now?

Extract from Noakes and Pridham (**8**(I), p. 158).

Documents

Hitler's plans for the army

On 28 February 1934 Hitler summoned the leaders of the SA and most of
the senior Reichswehr * generals. He promised to preserve the Reichswehr
and once again revealed his thinking on foreign policy. An account
survives in the unpublished memoirs of Field-Marshal von Weichs.*

...a militia as Röhm suggested would not be the least bit
suitable for national defence. He sought to establish this by
examples from military history. In the course of this he came to his
own experience. The hastily and superficially trained division to
which he belonged in 1914 as a private, had come to grief at
Langemarck with the most heavy losses. Therefore he was resolved
to raise a people's army, built up on the *Reichswehr*, rigorously
trained and equipped with the most modern weapons. He also
rejected a Fascist Militia on the Italian pattern. This new army
would have to be ready for any defence purposes after five years,
and after eight years suitable also for attacking. The SA must
confine itself to internal tasks....

Extract from O'Neill (**78**), pp. 40–1.

Hitler's life-style

As Hitler's architect Speer had a unique chance to observe the Führer's
inefficient work patterns.*

When, I would often ask myself, did he really work? Little was left
of the day; he rose late in the morning and conducted one or two
official conferences; but from the subsequent dinner on he more
or less wasted his time until the early hours of the evening. His rare
appointments in the late afternoon were imperilled by his passion
for looking at building plans. The adjutants often asked me:
'please don't show any plans today'. Then the drawings I had
brought with me would be left by the telephone switchboard at the
entrance and I would reply evasively to Hitler's enquiries.
Sometimes he would see through this game and would himself go
to look in the anteroom or the cloakroom for my roll of plans.
    In the eyes of the people Hitler was the Leader who watched
over the nation day and night. This was hardly so. But Hitler's lax

scheduling could be regarded as a life-style characteristic of the artistic temperament. According to my observations, he often allowed a problem to mature during the weeks when he seemed entirely taken up with trivial matters. Then after the 'sudden insight' came, he would spend a few days of intensive work giving final shape to his solution . . . . Once he had come to a decision, he relapsed again into his idleness.

Speer (**17**), p. 131.

The number of unemployed in millions
document 5

Year	January	July
1932	6.042	5.392
1933	6.014	4.464
1934	3.773	2.426
1935	2.974	1.754
1936	2.520	1.170
1937	1.853	0.563
1938	1.052	0.218
1939	0.302	0.038

Gebhardt, *Handbuch der Deutschen Geschichte*, 4, Union Verlag, 1959, p. 352.

The Four Year Plan
document 6

Hitler's memorandum was aimed at silencing economic objections, but it was also a clear statement of his basic philosophy and foreign policy intentions.

. . . Since the outbreak of the French Revolution, the world has been moving with ever increasing speed towards a new conflict, the most extreme solution of which is called Bolshevism, whose essence and aim, however, is solely the elimination of those strata of mankind which have hitherto provided the leadership and their replacement by world-wide Jewry.

No state will be able to withdraw or even remain at a distance from this historical conflict. Since Marxism, through its victory in Russia, has established one of the greatest empires in the world as a forward base for its future operations, this question has become a menacing one. Against a democratic world ideology rent within itself stands a unified aggressive will founded upon an authoritarian ideology. The means of military power available to this aggressive will are meantime increasing rapidly from year to year. One only has to compare the Red Army as it actually exists with the assumption of military men 10 or 15 years ago to realize the menacing extent of this development. Only consider the results of a further development over 10, 15 or 20 years and think what conditions will be like then!

Germany
Germany will, as always, have to be regarded as the focal point of the Western world in face of the Bolshevist attacks. I do not regard this as an agreeable mission but rather as a handicap and encumbrance upon our national life resulting from our position in Europe. We cannot, however, escape this destiny...

Extract from DGFP, Series C, vol. V, no. 490 (**6**), pp. 854–5.

document 7
Woman's place in the Nazi state

In his address to women at the Nuremberg party rally on 8 September 1934 Hitler summed up the Nazi view of the woman's position in society.

If one says that man's world is the State, his struggle, his readiness to devote his powers to the service of the community, one might be tempted to say that the world of woman is a smaller world. For her world is her husband, her family, her children and her house. But where would the greater world be if there were no one to care for the small world? ... Providence has entrusted to women the cares of that world which is peculiarly her own ....

Every child that a woman brings into the world is a battle, a battle waged for the existence of her people ....

Extract from Baynes, I (**3**), pp. 528–9.

document 8
A Nazi history syllabus

A model course for contemporary German history as recommended by the National Socialist Educator *(the official pedagogical paper in the Third Reich) for senior secondary children.*

Weeks	Subject	Relations to the Jews	Reading Material
1–4	Pre-war Germany, the Class-War, Profits, Strikes.	The Jew at large!	Hauptmann's The Weavers.
5–8	From Agrarian to Industrial State. Colonies.	The peasant in the claws of the Jew!	Descriptions of the colonies from Hermann Löns.
9–12	Conspiracy against Germany, encirclement, barrage around Germany	The Jew reigns! War plots.	Beumelburg: Barrage.... Life of Hindenburg, Wartime Letters.
13–16	German struggle – German want. Blockade! Starvation!	The Jew Becomes Prosperous! Profit from German want.	Manke: Espionage at the Front. War Reports.
17–20	The Stab in the Back. Collapse.	Jews as Leaders of the November insurrection.	Pierre des Granges: On Secret Service in Enemy Country. Bruno Brehm: That was the End.
21–24	Gemany's Golgotha. Erzberger's Crimes! Versailles.	Jews enter Germany from the East. Judah's . triumph.	Volkmann: Revolution over Germany. Feder: The Jews. The Stürmer newspaper.
25–28	Adolf Hitler. National Socialism.	Judah's Foe!	Mein Kampf. Dietrich Eckart.
29–32	The bleeding frontiers. Enslavement of Germany. The Volunteer Corps. Schlageter.	The Jew profits by Germany's misfortunes. Loans (Dawes, Young).	Beumelburg: Germany in Chains. Wehner: Pilgrimage to Paris. Schlageter – a German hero.
33–36	National Socialism at grips with crime and the underworld.	Jewish instigators of murder. The Jewish press.	Horst Wessel.
37–40	Germany's Youth at the Helm! The Victory of Faith.	The last fight against Judah.	Herbert Norkus. Reich Party The Congress.

Extract from Brady (**55**), p. 112.

Population statistics

Year	No. of marriages	Live births
1932	516,793	933,126
1933	638,573	971,174
1934	740,165	1,198,350
1935	651,435	1,263,976
1936	609,631	1,277,052
1937	618,971	1,275,212

Guillebaud (**88**), p. 275.

The egalitarian state

In a speech made in Berlin on 1 May 1937 Hitler claims to have broken with the old class system.

We in Germany have really broken with a world of prejudices. I leave myself out of account. I, too, am a child of the people; I do not trace my line from any castle: I come from the workshop. Neither was I a general: I was simply a soldier, as were millions of others. It is something wonderful that amongst us an unknown from the army of the millions of German people – of workers and of soldiers – could rise to be head of the Reich and of the nation. By my side stand Germans from all walks of life who today are amongst the leaders of the nation: men who once were workers on the land are now governing German states in the name of the Reich.... It is true that men who came from the bourgeoisie and former aristocrats have their place in this Movement. But to us it matters nothing whence they come if only they can work to the profit of our people. That is the decisive test. We have not broken down classes in order to set new ones in their place: we have broken down classes to make way for the German people as a whole.

Extract from Baynes, I (**3**), pp. 620–1.

Hitler and the Jews

(**a**) *In a speech delivered to the Reichstag* on 30 January 1939 Hitler specifically warned the Jews of their fate should war break out.*

Today I will once more be a prophet: If the international Jewish financiers in and outside Europe should succeed in plunging the nations into a world war, then the result will not be bolshevization of the earth and thus the victory of Jewry, but the annihilation of the Jewish race in Europe!

Extract from Baynes, 1 (**3**), p. 741.

(**b**) *In February 1941 both Göring and the Reich Ministry of Labour were pressing for the employment of eastern European Jews in the German war industries, but this was vetoed by Hitler. On 22 April 1941 an official of the Reich Ministry for Armaments and Munitions issued this statement:*

Following a directive from the Führer...there should be no attempt to transfer Jews from the east to the Reich for use as labour.

It is thus no longer possible to contemplate using Jews as replacements for labour which has been withdrawn, particularly from the building sector and from textile plants.

Extract from Noakes and Pridham (**8**(III), p. 1084).

document 12

Hitler's thinking on foreign policy in *Mein Kampf*

(**a**) *Hitler is quite specific about Germany's need for* Lebensraum* *or settlements in Russia.*

And so we National Socialists consciously draw a line beneath the foreign policy tendency of our pre-War period. We take up where we broke off six hundred years ago. We stop the endless German movement to the south and west, and turn our gaze towards the land in the east. At long last we break off the colonial and commercial policy of the pre-War period and shift to the soil policy of the future. If we speak of soil in Europe, we can primarily have in mind only Russia and her vassal border states.

Adolf Hitler, *Mein Kampf* (**1**), p. 598.

(**b**) *Hitler also advocated alliances with Britain and Italy against France.*

101

Anyone who undertakes an examination of the present alliance possibilities for Germany from the above standpoint must arrive at the conclusion that the last practicable tie remains with England .... We must not close our eyes to the fact that a necessary interest on the part of England in the annihilation of Germany no longer exists today; that, on the contrary, England's policy from year to year must be directed more and more to an obstruction of France's unlimited drive for hegemony....

And Italy, too, cannot and will not desire a further reinforcement of the French position of superior power in Europe....

Adolf Hitler, *Mein Kampf* (1), pp. 564–6.

(c) *In criticising Wilhelmine foreign policy for pursuing too many goals at once Hitler outlines an alternative programme which Hillgruber and Hildebrand argue he covertly adopted in the 1930s.*

The correct road would even then have been the third: a strengthening of our continental power by gaining new soil in Europe, and precisely this seemed to place a completion by later acquisitions of colonial territory within the realm of the naturally possible. This policy, to be sure, could only have been carried out in alliance with England or with so abnormal an emphasis on the military implements of power that for forty or fifty years cultural tasks would have been forced into the background.

Adolf Hitler, *Mein Kampf* (1), p. 558.

document 13

The Hossbach memorandum

On 5 November 1937 Hitler called a meeting of his most important ministers and service chiefs. An account of the meeting was compiled some five days later by Hitler's adjutant, Colonel Hossbach, which in 1946 was accepted by the Nuremberg Tribunal as a 'blueprint' of Hitler's intentions to wage war.

...His [Hitler's] exposition to follow was the fruit of thorough deliberation and the experience of his four-and-a-half years of power... and [he] asked, in the interest of a long-term German policy, that his exposition be regarded, in the event of death, as his last will and testament.

The *Führer* then continued:

The aim of German policy was to make secure and to preserve the racial community and to enlarge it. It was therefore a question of spac....

The question for Germany was: Where could she achieve the greatest gain at the lowest cost? German policy had to reckon with two hate-inspired antagonists, Britain and France, to whom a German colossus in the centre of Europe was a thorn in the flesh, and both countries were opposed to any further strengthening of Germany's position either in Europe or overseas....

Germany's problem could only be solved by the use of force, and this was never without attendant risk. The Silesian campaigns of Frederick the Great, Bismarck's wars against Austria and France, had involved unheard-of risks, and the swiftness of Prussian action in 1870 had kept Austria from entering the war. If the resort to force with its attendant risks is accepted as the basis of the following exposition, then there remains still to be answered the questions 'When?' and 'How?' In this matter there were three contingencies to be dealt with:

Contingency 1: Period 1943–45
After this date only a change for the worse, from our point of view, could be expected.

The equipment of the Army, Navy and *Luftwaffe*, as well as the formation of the officer corps, was nearly completed. Equipment and armament were modern; in further delay there lay the danger of their obsolescence.... Our relative strength would decrease in relation to the rearmament, which would by then have been carried out by the rest of the world. If we did not act by 1943–45 any year could, owing to a lack of reserves, produce the food crisis, to cope with which the necessary foreign exchange was not available, and this must be regarded as a 'waning point of the regime'. Besides, the world was expecting our attack and was increasing its counter measures from year to year. It was while the rest of the world was still fencing itself off that we were obliged to take the offensive. Nobody knew today what the situation would be in the years 1943–45. One thing was certain, that we could wait no longer.... If the *Führer* was still living, it was his unalterable determination to solve Germany's problem of space by 1943–45 at the latest....

Contingency 2
If internal strife in France should develop into such a domestic

crisis as to absorb the French army completely and render it incapable of use for war against Germany, then the time for action against the Czechs would have come.

Contingency 3
If France should be so embroiled in war with another State that she could not 'proceed' against Germany.

For the improvement of our politico-military position our first objective, in the event of our being embroiled in war, must be to overthrow Czechoslovakia and Austria simultaneously in order to remove the threat to our flank in any possible operation against the West....

The *Führer* saw contingency 3 coming definitely nearer; it might emerge from the present tensions in the Mediterranean, and he was resolved to take advantage of it whenever it happened, even as early as 1938.

In the light of past experience, the *Führer* saw no early end to the hostilities in Spain....

Extract from DGFP, Series D, vol. I (**6**), pp. 29–38.

document 14
Hitler takes the decision to attack Russia

Hitler saw the defeat of Russia as the key to defeating Britain and to keeping America out of the war. General Halder recorded Hitler's assessment of the military and diplomatic situation at a military conference on 31 July 1940.

Führer:
(a) Stresses his scepticism regarding technical feasibility [of an invasion of Britain]; however satisfied with results produced by Navy.
(b) Emphasizes weather factor.
(c) Discusses enemy resources for counteraction. Our small Navy is only 15 per cent of enemy's.... In any decision we must bear in mind that if we take risks, the prize too is high.
(d) In the event that invasion does not take place, our action must be directed to eliminate all factors that let England hope for a change in the situation. To all intents and purposes the war is won.... Submarine and air warfare may bring about a final

decision, but this may be one or two years off. Britain's hope lies in Russia and the United States. If Russia drops out of the picture, America too is lost for Britain, because elimination of Russia would tremendously increase Japan's power in the Far East.

Russia is the Far Eastern sword of Britain and the United States pointed at Japan.... Japan has her programme which she wants to carry through before the end of the war....

With Russia smashed, Britain's last hope would be shattered. Germany will then be master of Europe and the Balkans. Decision: Russia's destruction must therefore be made part of this struggle. Spring 1941. The sooner Russia is crushed, the better. Attack achieves its purpose only if Russian state can be shattered to its roots with one blow.... Holding part of the country alone will not do. Standing still for the following winter would be perilous. So it is better to wait a little longer but with resolute determination to eliminate Russia....

Extract from Noakes and Pridham (8) (1974 edition pp. 586–7).

document 15
German treatment of Russian prisoners of war

The ordinary Russian soldier was treated abominably by the Germans during the winter of 1941–42. Between June 1941 and February 1942 more than two million died of starvation and maltreatment. However, belatedly the economic pressures of total war forced Hitler to tolerate their employment in the German war industries. The following eye-witness report gives an account of treatment of Russian troops at the Prisoners' Camp at Blizin, near Skarzysko, Poland.

The camp consists of four huts, situated in the fields near the village, so that everything that happens there can be observed by the neighbours. Train-loads of prisoners which arrived here had taken over a fortnight to reach the new camp and were without food or water. Each wagon when opened contained scores of dead bodies. The sick who could not move were thrown out. They were ordered to sit down on the ground near the camp and were shot by the S.S.-men before the eyes of the rest. The camp contains about 2,500 prisoners. The average daily death-rate is about 50. The dead bodies are thrown out on to the fields and sprinkled with lime, often lying some days after that unburied.... The prisoners received ¼ kg of bread made of horse-chestnut flour and potato-skins, and soup made of rotten cabbage....

Extract from *German Crimes in Poland* i–ii, Warsaw, 1946, pp. 268–9.

document 16

Resettlement policies in Poland

Goebbels comments on the adverse economic and political effects of Himmler's resettlement policies in the Lublin area in 1943. Ernst Zoerner was an old guard Nazi who had been appointed Mayor of Dresden in 1933.

Zoerner has resigned as governor of Lublin. He called on me to give the reasons for his resignation. He had succeeded on the whole in squeezing an unusual amount of food out of the Lublin district. Understandably so, for this district is the most fertile in the entire General Government. Suddenly, however, he received orders for resettlement that had a very bad effect upon morale. Some 50,000 Poles were to be evacuated to begin with. Our police were able to grab only 25,000; the other 25,000 joined the partisans. It isn't hard to imagine what consequences that had for the whole area. Now he was to evacuate about 190,000 more Poles. This he refused to do, and in my opinion he was right. His district will now be governed from Warsaw by Governor Dr Fischer. Although Dr Frank, the Governor General, agreed with Zoerner's views he hasn't sufficient authority to put his foot down on the encroachments of the police and the S.S. It makes you want to tear out your hair when you encounter such appalling political ineptitude. At home we are waging total war with all its consequences and are subordinating all philosophical and ideological aims to the supreme aim of final victory: in the occupied areas, however, things are done as though we were living in profound peace....

Extract from *The Goebbels Diaries* (**10**), pp. 313–14.

document 17

Hitler retains his charisma in March 1945

Speer was desperately trying to persuade the Gauleiters* to defy Hitler's orders to destroy German industrial plants before Allied troops arrived. To *his surprise he still found reserves of optimism and confidence that Hitler would save Germany.*

I drove to the Ruhr area once more. Saving its industry was the crucial question for the post-war era. In Westphalia a flat tyre forced us to stop. Unrecognized in the twilight I stood in a farm-yard talking to farmers. To my surprise, the faith in Hitler which had been hammered into their minds all these last years was still strong. Hitler could never lose the war, they declared. 'The Führer is still holding something in reserve that he'll play at the last moment. Then the turning point will come. It's only a trap, his letting the enemy come so far into our country.' Even among members of the government I still encountered this naïve faith in deliberately withheld secret weapons that at the last moment would annihilate an enemy recklessly advancing into the country. Funk [the Economics Minister], for example, asked me: 'We still have a special weapon, don't we? A weapon that will change everything?'

Speer (**17**), p. 446.

document 18

German public opinion during the war

The Security Service of the SS* prepared regular and objective reports on the public mood in Germany. By the summer of 1944 they were discontinued because they made such depressing reading!

(**a**) *Report of 7 October 1940*
Grudgingly and reluctantly the population is getting used to the thought of a second winter of war, and daily worries, particularly about fuel, have come to the surface. The thought frequently comes up that the Tripartite Pact shows that the war has been enormously extended. . . .

(**b**) *Report of 8 July 1943*
The telling of vulgar jokes detrimental to the State, even about the *Führer* himself, has increased considerably since Stalingrad. In conversations in cafés, factories and other meeting places people tell each other the 'latest' political jokes and in many cases make no distinction between those with a harmless content and those which are clearly in opposition to the state. . . .

Extract from Noakes and Pridham (**8**) (1974 edition), pp. 654–69.

document 19

Gross national product and military expenditure in Germany, the USA and Britain, 1933–45

Year	Germany (billions RM)			USA (billions $)			Britain (billions £)		
	GNP	Mil. expend.	Per cent	GNP	Mil. expend.	Per cent	Nat. income	Mil. expend.	Per cent
1933	59	1.9	3	56	0.5	1	3.7	0.1	3
1934	67	4.1	6	65	0.7	1	3.9	0.1	3
1935	74	6.0	8	73	0.9	1	4.1	0.1	2
1936	83	10.9	13	83	0.9	1	4.4	0.2	5
1937	93	11.7	13	91	1.0	1	4.6	0.3	7
1938	105	17.2	17	85	1.0	1	4.8	0.4	8
1939	130	30.0	23	91	1.3	1	5.0	1.1	22
1940	141	53.0	38	101	2.2	2	6.0	3.2	53
1941	152	71.0	47	126	13.8	11	6.8	4.1	60
1942	165	91.0	55	159	49.6	31	7.5	4.8	64
1943	184	112.0	61	193	80.4	42	8.0	5.0	63
1944				211	88.6	42	8.2	5.1	62
1945				214	75.9	36	8.3	4.4	53

Carroll (**84**), p. 184.

document 20

Individual acts of opposition

Many Germans defied the Nazi regime by hiding Jews. In Berlin, for example, some 5,000 survived thanks to such efforts. Below is an extract from the account of a German-Jewish woman.

I was constantly sent for by the Gestapo. In 1942 these interrogation sessions became even more threatening and I therefore went underground. In the middle of May 1942 I went to Silesia and stayed in several places without officially registering myself. I lived in Breslau, Gleiwitz, Hindenburg, in the countryside and in Spahlitz (in the district of Oels). It was here that I remained hidden for months at the house of a German lawyer.... (Later after I was arrested this brave man had another Jewish woman hidden in his house) ...

Wiener Library, Eye Witness Accounts, PIIc, no. 153.

Glossary and Abbreviations

Alte Kämpfer	The veterans of the Nazi Party
Anschluss	Incorporation of Austria into Germany, 1938
Blitzkrieg	A lightning war
Führer	Leader
*Gau (*pl. *Gaue)*	A region or province
Gauleiter	Regional party leader
Gleichschaltung	Coordination or streamlining. The process of putting everything under Nazi control
Jungmädel	The junior section of the German Girls' League
Jungvolk	The junior section of the Hitler Youth
Junker	Prussian nobleman and landowner
Kampfbund	The Patriotic Combat Leagues
Landtag	A provincial Diet
Lebensraum	Living space
Luftwaffe	Air force
Mein Kampf	My Struggle
Ministerpräsident	Federal state president or prime minister (cf. a US state governor)
Mittelstand	Middle class
Ordensburg	Finishing school for the future Nazi elite
Putsch	A revolt or coup
Rechtsstaat	Constitutional state
Regierungspräsident	District president
Reichsbank	The German national bank
Reichskirche	The German national church
Reichskommissar	Reich Commissioner
Reichsrat	The upper house of the German parliament
Reichstag	The lower house of the German parliament
Reichswehr	The German army (not in official use after 1935)
Stahlhelm	The right-wing ex-soldiers' league (literally 'steel helmet')
Stufenplan	A plan carried out by stages

Glossary and Abbreviations

Völkisch	Ethnic and national
Volkssturm	A conscript home-guard
Wehrmacht	The German army
Gestapo	(*Geheime Staatspolizei*) Secret State Police
KPD	(*Kommunistische Partei Deutschlands*) German Communist Party
NSDAP	(*Nationalsozialistische Deutsche Arbeiterpartei*) National Socialist German Workers' Party
RKFDV	(*Reichskommissar für die Festigung des Deutschen Volkstums*) Reich Commissioner for the Strengthening of the German Race
SA	(*Sturmabteilung*) Storm or assault troops
SD	(*Sicherheitsdienst*) Security service of the SS
SPD	(*Sozialistische Partei Deutschlands*) German Social Democratic Party
SS	(*Schutzstaffel*) Elite guard (literally, protection squad)
Waffen SS	Armed or militarised SS

Bibliography

This is inevitably only a limited selection of literature on the Third Reich. As far as possible I have tried to include works in English which are easily available.

DOCUMENTS
(a) *Works and speeches of Adolf Hitler*
1 *Mein Kampf,* ed. D. Watt, Hutchinson, 1977.
2 *Hitler's Secret Book,* ed. T. Taylor, Grove Press, 1961.
3 *Hitler's Speeches,* 1922–39, 2 vols, ed. Baynes, N. Oxford University Press, 1942.
4 *Hitler's Table Talk,* with an introductory essay, 'The Mind of Adolf Hitler', by H.R. Trevor-Roper, Weidenfeld & Nicolson, 1953.

(b) *General document collections*
5 Boelcke, W., *The Secret Conferences of Dr Goebbels,* Weidenfeld & Nicolson, 1967.
6 *Documents on German Foreign Policy, 1918–1945,* Series C (1933–37), Series D (1937–41), HM Stationery Office, 1950–.
7 Hofer, W., *Der Nationalsozialismus. Dokumente, 1933–45,* Fischer, 1957.
8 Noakes, J. and Pridham, G., *Nazism, 1919–1945,* vol. I, *The Rise to Power,* vol. II, *State, Economy and Society, 1933–39,* vol. III, *Foreign Policy, War and Racial Extermination,* vol. IV, *Germany at War: The Home Front, 1939–45,* Exeter University Press, 1983–.
9 The Trial of the Major War Criminals before the International Military Tribunal, *Proceedings,* vols I–XXIII; *Documents in Evidence,* vols XXIV–XLII, HM Stationery Office, 1947–49.

DIARIES AND MEMOIRS
10 *The Goebbels Diaries,* Hamish Hamilton, 1948.

11 *The von Hassell Diaries*, 1938–44, Doubleday, 1947.
12 Meinecke, F., *The German Catastrophe: Reflections and Recollections*, Harvard University Press, 1950.
13 von Papen, F., *Memoirs*, Deutsch, 1952.
14 Rauschning, H., *Hitler Speaks. A Series of Political Conversations with Adolf Hitler and his Real Aims*, Thornton Butterworth, 1939.
15 Schacht, H., *My First Seventy-Six Years*, Allan Wingate, 1955.
16 Schmidt, P., *Hitler's Interpreter*, Heinemann, 1951.
17 Speer, A., *Inside the Third Reich*, Weidenfeld & Nicolson, 1970.

BACKGROUND HISTORY

18 Berghahn, V., *Germany and the Approach of War in 1914*, Macmillan, 1973.
19 Blackbourn, D. and Eley, G., *Peculiarities of German History* (trans.), Oxford University Press, 1984.
20 Broszat, M., *Hitler and the Collapse of Weimar Germany* (trans.), Berg, 1987.
21 Carsten, F.L., *The Rise of Fascism*, Batsford, 1967.
22 Craig, G.A., *Germany, 1866–1945*, Oxford University Press, 1978.
23 Hales, E., *The Catholic Church in the Modern World*, Eyre & Spottiswoode, 1958.
24 Heiden, K., *A History of National Socialism*, Methuen, 1971.
25 Hiden, J. W., *The Weimar Republic*, Longman, 1974.
26 Holborn, H., *A History of Modern Germany, 1840–1945*, Eyre & Spottiswoode, 1969.
27 Kohn, H., *The Mind of Germany*, Macmillan, 1961.
28 Laqueur, W. ed., *Fascism. A Reader's Guide*, Penguin, 1976.
29 Mosse, G.L., *The Crisis of German Ideology. Intellectual Origins of the Third Reich*, Weidenfeld & Nicolson, 1964.
30 Nicholls, A.J., *Weimar and the Rise of Hitler*, Macmillan, 1968.
31 Nolte, E., *Three Faces of Fascism: Action Française, Italian Fascism, National Socialism*, Mentor, 1969.
32 Pridham, G., *Hitler's Rise to Power. The Nazi Movement in Bavaria, 1923–33*, Hart-Davis, MacGibbon, 1973.
33 Stern, F., *The Politics of Cultural Despair: A Study in the Rise of the Germanic Ideology*, University of California Press, 1974.

34 Taylor, A.J.P., *The Course of German History*, Methuen, 1961.
35 Trevor-Roper, H.R., 'The Phenomenon of Fascism', in *European Fascism*, ed. Woolf, S.J., Weidenfeld & Nicolson, 1970.
36 Vermeil, E., *Germany's Three Reichs. Their History and Culture*, Dakers, 1945.
37 Wehler, H-U., *The German Empire, 1871–1918* (trans.), Berg, 1984.

BIOGRAPHICAL STUDIES OF HITLER

38 Bullock, A., *Hitler. A Study in Tyranny*, Odhams, 1952; Penguin, 1962.
39 Carr, W., *Hitler. A Study in Personality and Politics*, Arnold, 1978.
40 Fest, J.C., *Hitler*, Weidenfeld & Nicolson, 1974; Penguin, 1977.
41 Heiden, K., *Der Führer. Hitler's Rise to Power*, Gollancz, 1944.
42 Jetzinger, F., *Hitler's Youth*, with a foreword by Alan Bullock, Hutchinson, 1958.
43 Kershaw, I., *Hitler*, Longman, 1991.
44 Maser, W., *Hitler*, Allen Lane, 1973.
45 Stone, N., *Hitler*, Hodder, 1980.
46 Watt, D.C., 'New Light on Hitler's Youth', *History Today*, vol. VIII, January 1958.
47 Watt, D.C., 'Hitler's Apprenticeship', *History Today*, vol. IX, November 1959.

THE NAZI TAKE-OVER OF POWER

48 Allan, W.S., *The Nazi Seizure of Power: The Experience of a Single Town, 1930–35*, Eyre & Spottiswoode, 1966.
49 Bracher, K.D., Sauer, W. and Schulz, G., *Die National-sozialistische Machtergreifung*, Westdeutscher Verlag, 1962.
50 Mommsen, H., 'The Reichstag Fire and its Political Consequences', in *Aspects of the Third Reich, 1933–45*, ed., Koch, H.W., Macmillan, 1985.
51 Tobias, F., *The Reichstag Fire*, Putnam, 1964.
52 Wheaton, E.B., *Prelude to Calamity: The Nazi Revolution 1933–35 with a Background Survey of the Weimar Era*, Gollancz, 1968.
53 Winkler, H., 'German Society, Hitler and the Illusion of

Restoration 1930–33', *Journal of Contemporary History*, vol. II, no. 4, October 1976.

GENERAL ACCOUNTS OF THE THIRD REICH

54 Bracher, K., *The German Dictatorship: The Origins, Structure and Consequences of National Socialism*, Weidenfeld & Nicolson, 1971; Penguin, 1973.

55 Brady, R.A., *The Spirit and Structure of German Fascism*, with a foreword by H.J. Laski, Gollancz, 1937.

56 Fest, J., *The Face of the Third Reich*, Weidenfeld & Nicolson, 1970; Penguin, 1979.

57 Frei, N., *National Socialist Rule in Germany: The Fuhrer State, 1933–45*, Blackwell, 1993.

58 Haffner, S., *Germany: Jekyll and Hyde*, Secker & Warburg, 1940.

59 Hildebrand, K. *The Third Reich* (trans.), Routledge, 1984.

60 Neumann, F., *Behemoth: The Structure and Practice of National Socialism*, Cass, 1967 (1st edn, 1942).

61 Rauschning, H., *Germany's Revolution of Destruction*, Heinemann, 1939.

62 Stern, J., *Hitler, the Führer and the People*, Fontana, 1975.

(a) The Party (including the SS and SA), the State and the Constitution

63 Bramsted, E.K., *Goebbels and National Socialist Propaganda, 1922–45*, Cresset Press, 1965.

64 Broszat, M., *The Hitler State. The Foundation and Development of the Internal Structure of the Third Reich*, Longman, 1981.

65 Buchheim, H. *et al. Anatomy of the SS State*, Collins, 1968.

66 Caplan, J., 'Bureaucracy, Politics and the National Socialist State', in *The Shaping of the Nazi State*, ed. Stachura, P.D., Croom Helm, 1978.

67 Gellateley, R., *The Gestapo and German Society*, Oxford University Press, 1990.

68 Koehl, R.L., *The Black Corps: The Structure and Power Struggles of the Nazi SS*, University of Wisconsin Press, 1983.

69 Mau, H., 'Die Zweite Revolution der 30 Juni 1934', *Vierteljahresheft für Zeitgeschichte*, no. 1 (1953).

70 Mommsen, H. *Beamtentum im Dritten Reich*, Deutsche Verlags-Anstalt, 1966.

71 Mommsen, H., 'National Socialism: Continuity and

Change', in *Fascism*, ed. Laqueur, W., Wildwood House, 1976; Penguin, 1979.

72 Noakes, J., *Government, Party and People in Nazi Germany*, Exeter University Press, 1980.

73 Orlow, D., *The History of the Nazi Party*, vol. I, *1919–1933*, vol. II, *1933–1945*, David & Charles, 1971–73.

74 Peterson, E.N., *The Limits of Hitler's Power*, Princeton University Press, 1969.

75 Reitlinger, G., *The SS: Alibi of a Nation, 1922–45*, Viking, 1968.

76 Steiner, J., *Power Politics and Social Change in National Socialist Germany. A Process of Escalation into Mass Destruction*, Mouton, 1975.

(b) The Third Reich and the Army

77 Craig, G., *The Politics of the Prussian Army*, Oxford University Press, 1955.

78 O'Neill, R.J., *The German Army and the Nazi Party*, Cassell, 1966.

79 Seaton, A., *The German Army, 1933–45*, Weidenfeld & Nicolson, 1982.

80 Wheeler-Bennett, J.W., *The Nemesis of Power: The German Army in Politics, 1918–45*, Macmillan, 1961.

ECONOMIC AND SOCIAL HISTORY

81 Bessel, R., ed., *Life in the Third Reich*, Oxford University Press, 1987.

82 Bry, G., *Wages in Germany, 1871–1945*, Princeton University Press, 1960.

83 Burleigh, M. and Wippermann, W., *The Racial State: Germany 1933–45*, Cambridge University Press, 1991.

84 Carroll, B., *Total War: Aims and Economics in the Third Reich*, Mouton, 1968.

85 Conway, J.S., *The Nazi Persecution of the Churches, 1933–45*, Weidenfeld & Nicolson, 1968.

86 Dahrendorf, F., *Society and Democracy in Germany*, Doubleday, 1967.

87 Farquharson, J.E., *The Plough and the Swastika. The NSDAP and Agriculture in Germany, 1928–45*, Sage, 1976.

88 Guillebaud, C.W., *The Economic Recovery of Germany from 1933 to the Incorporation of Austria in March, 1938*, Macmillan, 1939.

89 Grünberger, R., *A Social History of the Third Reich*, Weidenfeld & Nicolson, 1971; Penguin, 1974.

90 Homze, E.L., *Foreign Labor in Germany*, Princeton University Press, 1967.

91 Kirkpatrick, C., *Nazi Germany: Its Women and Family Life*, Bobbs-Merrill, 1938.

92 Klein, B.H., *Germany's Economic Preparations for War*, Harvard University Press, 1959.

93 Koonz, C., *Women, the Family and Nazi Politics*, St Martin's Press, 1987.

94 Mason, T., 'Labour in the Third Reich, 1933–39', *Past and Present*, XXXIII, 1966.

95 Mason, T., 'Women in Germany, 1925–1940 (Family, Welfare and Work. Part I)', *History Workshop*, I, Spring 1976.

96 Milward, A.S., *The German Economy at War*, Athlone Press, 1965.

97 Overy, R.J., *The Nazi Economic Recovery, 1932–38*, Macmillan, 1982.

98 Overy, R.J., 'Blitzkriegswirtschaft?' *Vierteljahreshefte für Zeitgeschichte*, vol. 36, 1988.

99 Overy, R.J., 'Hitler's War Plans and the German Economy', in *Paths to War*, ed. Boyce, R. and Robertson, E.M., Macmillan, 1989.

100 Petzina, D., *Autarkiepolitik im Dritten Reich. Der national-sozialistische Vierjahresplan*, Deutsche Verlags-Anstalt, 1968.

101 Rabinbach, A.G., 'The Aesthetics of Production in the Third Reich', *Journal of Contemporary History*, vol. 11, no. 4, October 1976.

102 Schoenbaum, D., *Hitler's Social Revolution*, Weidenfeld & Nicolson, 1967.

103 Schweitzer, A., *Big Business in the Third Reich*, Eyre & Spottiswoode, 1964.

104 Seydewitz, M., *Civil Life in Wartime Germany. The Story of the Home Front*, Viking, 1945.

105 Steinert, M., *Hitler's War and the Germans. Public Mood and Attitude during the Second World War*, Ohio University Press, 1977.

106 Stephenson, J., 'Girls' Higher Education in Germany in the 1930s', *Journal of Contemporary History*, vol. 10, no. 1, 1975.

107 Stephenson, J.S., *Women in German Society*, Croom Helm, 1975.

FOREIGN POLICY

108 Bell, P.M.H., *The Origins of the Second World War in Europe*, Longman, 1986.

109 Bullock, A., 'Hitler and the Origins of the Second World War', in *The Origins of the Second World War*, ed. Robertson, E.M., Macmillan, 1971.

110 Carr, W.M., *Arms, Autarky and Aggression*, Edward Arnold, 1972.

111 Carr, W.M., 'National Socialism: Foreign Policy and Wehrmacht', in *Fascism*, ed. Laqueur, W., Wildwood House, 1976; Penguin, 1979.

112 Cecil, R., *Hitler's Decision to Invade Russia*, Davis-Poynter, 1975.

113 Dallin, A., *German Rule in Russia, 1941–45*, Macmillan, 1957.

114 Hiden, J., *Germany and Europe, 1919–39*, 2nd edn, Longman, 1993.

115 Hildebrand, K., *The Foreign Policy of the Third Reich*, Batsford, 1973.

116 Hillgruber, A., *Hitlers Strategie, Politik und Kriegsführung, 1940–1941*, Bernard & Graefe, 1965.

117 Hillgruber, A., 'England's Place in Hitler's Plans for World Dominion', *Journal of Contemporary History*, vol. 9, no. 1, January 1974.

118 Irving, D., *Hitler's War*, Viking, 1977.

119 Koch, H.W., 'Hitler and the Origins of the Second World War: Second Thoughts on the Status of Some of the Documents', in *The Origins of the Second World War*, ed. Robertson, E.M., Macmillan, 1971.

120 Koch, H.W., '"The Spectre of a Separate Peace in the East": Russo-German Peace Feelers, 1942–44', *Journal of Contemporary History*, vol. 10, no. 3, July 1975.

121 Koch, H.W., 'Hitler's Programme and the Genesis of Operation Barbarossa', in *Aspects of the Third Reich*, ed. Koch, H.W., Macmillan, 1985.

122 Koehl, R.L., *RKFDV: German Resettlement and Population Policy, 1939–1945*, Harvard University Press, 1957.

123 Martel, G., *The Origins of the Second World War Reconsidered*, Allen & Unwin, 1986.

124 Mason, T., 'Some Origins of the Second World War', in *The Origins of the Second World War*, ed. Robertson, E.M., Macmillan, 1971.

125 Michalka, W., 'From the Anti-Comintern Pact to the Euro-Asiatic Bloc: Ribbentrop's Alternative Concept to Hitler's Foreign Policy Programme', in *Aspects of the Third Reich*, ed. Koch, H.W., Macmillan, 1985.

126 Rich, N., *Hitler's War Aims*, 2 vols., Deutsch, 1973–74.

127 Robertson, E.M., ed., *The Origins of the Second World War*, Macmillan, 1971.

128 Robertson, E.M., 'Hitler Turns from the West to Russia, May–December, 1940', in *Paths to War*, ed. Boyce, R. and Robertson, E.M., Macmillan, 1989.

129 Seabury, P., *The Wilhelmsstrasse. A Study of German Diplomats under the Nazi Regime*, University of California Press, 1954.

130 Smelser, R.M., *The Sudeten Problem 1933–38. Volkstumspolitik and the Formation of Nazi Foreign Policy*, Dawson, 1971.

131 Taylor, A.J.P., *The Origins of the Second World War*, Hamish Hamilton, 1961.

132 Thies, J., 'Hitler's European Building Programme', *Journal of Contemporary History*, vol. 13, no. 3, July 1978.

133 Thorne, C., *The Approach of War*, Macmillan, 1967.

134 Watt, D.C., 'Hitler's Visit to Rome and the May Weekend Crisis: A Study in Hitler's Response to External Stimuli', *Journal of Contemporary History*, vol. 9, no. 1, January 1974.

135 Watt, D.C., *How War Came*, Heinemann, 1989.

136 Weinberg, G.L., *Germany and the Soviet Union, 1939–41*, Brill, 1954.

137 Weinberg, G.L., *The Foreign Policy of Hitler's Germany*, vol. 1, *Diplomatic Revolution in Europe, 1933–36*, vol. II, *Starting World War II, 1937–39*, University of Chicago Press, 1970–80.

138 Wiskemann, E., *The Rome–Berlin Axis*, Collins, 1966.

139 Wright, G., *The Ordeal of Total War, 1939–45*, Harper & Row, 1968.

THE GERMAN OPPOSITION

140 Bethge, E., *Bonhoeffer, Exile and Martyr*, Collins, 1975.

141 Graml, H., Mommsen, H. *et al. The German Resistance to Hitler*, Batsford, 1970.

142 Hoffmann, P., *The History of the German Resistance in Germany*, MacDonald and Janes, 1977.

143 Kershaw, I., *Popular Opinion and Popular Dissent in the Third Reich: Bavaria, 1933–45*, Oxford University Press, 1983.
144 Prittie, T., *Germans against Hitler*, Hutchinson, 1964.
145 Ritter, G., *The German Resistance: Carl Goerdeler's Struggle against Tyranny*, Allen & Unwin, 1958.
146 Rothfels, H., *The German Opposition to Hitler*, Oswald Wolff, 1961.
147 Zeller, E., *The Flame of Freedom: The Struggle against Hitler*, Oswald Wolff, 1967.

THE COLLAPSE OF THE THIRD REICH
148 Toland, J., *The Last Hundred Days*, Barker, 1966.
149 Trevor-Roper, H., *The Last Days of Hitler*, Macmillan, 1947.

ANTI-SEMITISM AND THE HOLOCAUST
150 Bankier, D., 'Hitler and the Policy-making Process on the Jewish Question', *Holocaust and Genocide Studies*, vol. III, no. 1, 1988.
151 Broszat, M., 'Hitler and the Genesis of the "Final Solution"', in *Aspects of the Third Reich*, ed. Koch, H.W. Macmillan, 1985.
152 Dawidowicz, L.S., *The War against the Jews, 1933–45*, Penguin (10th anniversary edn), 1986.
153 Fleming, G., *Hitler and the Final Solution*, Oxford University Press, 1986.
154 Fox, J., 'Holocaust as History', *Modern History Review*, vol. III, no. 2, 1991.
155 Graml, H., *Antisemitism in the Third Reich* (trans.), Blackwell, 1992.
156 Kettenacker, L., 'Hitler's Final Solution and its Rationalization', in *'The Führer State'. Myth and Reality: Studies on the Structure and Politics of the Third Reich*, ed. Hirschfeld, G. and Kettenacker, L., Kletta Cotta/German Historical Institute, London, 1981.
157 Levin, N., *The Holocaust: The Destruction of European Jewry, 1933–45*, Cromwell, 1968.
158 Marrus, M.R., 'The History of the Holocaust: A Survey of Recent Literature', *Journal of Modern History*, vol. 59, no. 1, 1987.
159 Mommsen, H., 'The Realization of the Unthinkable: The "Final Solution" of the Jewish Question in the Third Reich', in *'The Führer State'. Myth and Reality: Studies on the*

Structure and Politics of the Third Reich, ed. Hirschfeld, G. and Kettenacker, L., Kletta Cotta/German Historical Institute, London, 1981.

160 Schleunes, K.A., *The Twisted Road to Auschwitz. Nazi Policy towards German Jews*, Deutsch, 1972.

161 Yisraeli, D., 'The Third Reich and the Transfer Agreement', *Journal of Contemporary History*, vol. 6, no. 2, 1971.

THE THIRD REICH AND THE HISTORIANS

162 Evans, R., *In Hitler's Shadow: West German Historians and the Attempt to Escape from the Nazi Past*, Tauris, 1989.

163 Hiden, J. and Farquharson, J., *Explaining Hitler's Germany*, Batsford, 1983.

164 Kershaw, I., *The Nazi Dictatorship. Problems and Perspectives*, Arnold, 2nd edn, 1989.

165 Nolte, E., 'Between Myth and Revisionism? The Third Reich in the Perspective of the 1980's', in *Aspects of the Third Reich*, ed. Koch, H.W., Macmillan, 1985.

Index

Index

RELATED TITLES

Anthony Wood, *The Russian Revolution*
Second Edition (1986)   0 582 35559 1

This study provides a concise history of the Revolution and analyses the relationship between the various social theories of the revolutionaries and the later course of events. It traces the heated arguments amongst left-wing groups from the years before the fall of the monarchy up to the propounding of the New Economic Policy by Lenin in 1921, and concludes by considering why the Bolsheviks succeeded in seizing and retaining power.

R J Overy, *The Inter-War Crisis 1919-1939* (1994)   0 582 35379 3

This *Seminar Study* takes the reader through the tumultuous, uncertain years of the inter-war period. In it Richard Overy argues that the inter-war years were, at the time, perceived to be years of crisis across the world. The book seeks to explain why dictatorships came to supplant democracy - in Italy, Spain, Germany, the Baltic States, and the Balkans and why the world slid into war once more in 1939.

John Hiden, *The Weimar Republic*
Second Edition (1996)   0 582 28706 5

It is usually assumed that, thanks to the harsh terms of the Versailles Settlement, the Weimar Republic was doomed from the outset and that Hitler's rise to power was inevitable. In this succinct *Seminar Study* (now revised for the first time since 1974) Professor Hiden seeks to dispel this simplistic view. He examines the fundamental problems of the new state but also argues that it did make some progress in tackling the major political, social and economic problems facing it in the 1920s. The author concludes by showing how it was a complex interaction of many factors which finally brought Hitler to power.

Martin McCauley, *Stalin and Stalinism*
Second Edition (1995)   0 582 27658 6

Readers will welcome the Second Edition of one of the most popular books in the series. For the new edition the author re-examines the remarkable phenomenon of Stalin and "Stalinism" in the light of the latest research findings of the Russian archives. The book also takes into account the vigorous scholarly debate between the old, dominant totalitarian interpretation of Stalinism and the alternative school of thought put forward by the "social historians" in the 1980s.

Harry Browne, *Spain's Civil War*
Second Edition (1996)   0 582 28988 2

Harry Browne's accessible account of the Spanish Civil War has now been updated, and expanded, in the light of recent scholarship. In particular, there is now a fuller analysis of the politics of the Second Republic and the regional and social bases of Spain's political parties. There is also a more detailed account of the military conduct of the war, of the extent of international involvement, and of the means by which both sides, despite the Non-Intervention Agreement, were able to purchase arms abroad.

RJ Overy, *The Origins of the Second World War*
Second Edition (1998)   0 582 29085 6

The Second World War has usually been seen simply as Hitler's war and yet it was Britain and France who declared war on Germany not the other way round. In this hugely successful study Richard Overy offers a multi-national explanation of the outbreak of hostilities. For the new edition new material has been added on the Munich crisis and on Japan but the most significant change is to be found in the treatment of the Soviet Union. Since 1989 knowledge of Soviet foreign policy has been transformed, and this is reflected in a complete redrafting of the sections covering Soviet actions from the Czech crisis in 1938 to the final showdown with Germany in 1941.

Martin McCauley, *The Origins of the Cold War 1941-1949*
Second Edition (1995)   0 582 27659 4

This popular study explores the key questions facing students. Who was responsible for the Cold War? Was it inevitable? Was Stalin genuinely interested in a post-war agreement? For the Second Edition Martin McCauley has revised and expanded his original text in the light of recent events - the ending of the Cold War, the collapse of Communism and the demise of the USSR in 1991.

Martin McCauley, *The Khrushchev Era, 1953 - 1964*
(1995)   0 582 27776 0

In this new study Martin McCauley explores all aspects of the Khrushchev era: including reforms in agriculture, economic policy, uprisings in Eastern Europe, the Cuban Missile Crisis of 1962, de-Stalinisation and Khrushchev's attempts to reform the Communist Party. The book will be greatly welcomed by history and politics students alike.